GROWING OLD

Remember, there are no do-overs!
Grab life & enjoy!
God Bless
HWestover

GROWING OLD

ONE LUCILLE BALL MOMENT AT A TIME

HEATHER NUTTALL WESTOVER

NEW DEGREE PRESS

COPYRIGHT © 2022 HEATHER NUTTALL WESTOVER

All rights reserved.

GROWING OLD
One Lucille Ball Moment at a Time

ISBN 979-8-88504-086-0 *Paperback*
      979-8-88504-715-9 *Kindle Ebook*
      979-8-88504-194-2 *Ebook*

CONTENTS

	FOREWORD	7
	DEDICATION	9
CHAPTER 1	MY HELLO	11
CHAPTER 2	CUSSING ISN'T ALWAYS THE COOLEST	17
CHAPTER 3	JUST WHAT IS A LUCILLE BALL MOMENT ANYWAY	25
CHAPTER 4	SANDS THROUGH THE HOURGLASS	37
CHAPTER 5	THE "I HATE HEATHER NUTTALL CLUB"	45
CHAPTER 6	THINGS MY PARENTS TAUGHT ME	57
CHAPTER 7	BECOMING A RUNNER	65
CHAPTER 8	50-SOMETHINGS AND TATTOOS	77
CHAPTER 9	THE DAY THE MUSIC DIED	87
CHAPTER 10	THE SNAKE WRANGLER	99
CHAPTER 11	THE OBSTACLE COURSE CALLED HIGH SCHOOL	109
CHAPTER 12	EXPERIMENTING WITH SELF-CARE	121
CHAPTER 13	MAKING THINGS HAPPEN AFTER 50	131
CHAPTER 14	THE SECOND HALF OF MY LIFE	141
	ACKNOWLEDGMENTS	149
	APPENDIX	151

FOREWORD

Being married . . . it's like driving a car. It can be fun, exciting, comfortable, boring, terrifying, and you can never quite anticipate what's over the next hill. In our case, the journey started out on a gravel road. What gravel roads don't have are signs warning of dangerous conditions ahead—or even speed limits for that matter.

Our road was pretty bumpy. What no one warned me about was that married vehicles come equipped with two steering wheels. Two steering wheels and two people with different driving styles can make for a very eventful journey and at times, somewhat dangerous conditions. The trick to successfully driving this vehicle is to learn your copilot's style, strengths, weaknesses, and most importantly, to know when to remove your hands. If it's a blinding snow or rainstorm, I know I'm up: time to slow it down and be a bit cautious. Heather is more suited for a racetrack. When we head down that long stretch of interstate, I have learned to let go and maybe close my eyes at times. I know we'll cover the next one hundred miles in about twenty minutes or so. She is the souped-up race car I had no business getting ahold of before learning how to really care for something that wild.

Our road has become much smoother as we've gotten older. As I look through the rearview mirror, I'm reminded of all the adventures we've been on and the few detours we had to navigate. Now looking through the windshield, I'm reminded that the road ahead is much shorter than the road behind. It sure is nice to relax and enjoy the ride, maybe to take one hand off the wheel to hold the hand next to you.

She gave me veto rights to any story in this book, but I didn't need to use them. She's protective of our marriage and me, even while being brutally honest. When you read, know that these stories are both of our views coming together in one book. This is the story of our lives, told with my blessing.

To Heather:

I'm proud of you honey. I don't care how many books you sell, you're a best seller to me.

~Corey Westover

I'm not really sure I deserve him. There are still many ways we struggle to meet each other's needs if we aren't being intentional. Being able to look back over my life and say that I was never required to hand over my individuality, that I had the freedom to take care of us while at the same time taking care of me and still having a best friend since the age of thirteen is probably better than any trophy NASCAR could give me anyway. Thanks for everything Corey. ~Heather

PS, I can't believe you got me to willingly reference NASCAR.

DEDICATION

―

Delvin and Juanita Nuttall, there aren't enough words. You weren't perfect, and we struggled in what I now know to be perfectly normal ways. The parents this teenager thought had so much to learn turned out to be very worthy guides and mentors. Thank you.

Corey Westover, our girls, our boy, our grandkids, and all the souls who called us Mom and Dad in one form or another, you dominated the first half of my adult life and filled it with so much love and driven purpose. Thank you.

To all of the Gypsy and German bloodlines in the Nuttall and Bush heritage, well, you created one little perfect storm in this blue-eyed, hot-tempered wanderer. Thank you for all the generational pieces of courage I needed to keep going.

To the Sully Buttes Chargers, each family who made up the school system, each student, coach, teacher, and volunteer, in the eighties, we didn't really push very many options for girls. But I wouldn't have ever believed I could do anything without all of you who made me the woman I am today. All of my experiences, great and terrible, fed the fire in my soul to never give up. Thank you.

Andrea, thank you for stepping out of your comfort zone and approaching me that day at BOOMTOWN Pints & Pies. We had never met in person, but after watching my social media, you overcame your introverted tendencies and approached me that day. You are the match that finally lit my fire to make this first book happen. I won't let you down, and this one isn't the last.

To every soul who ever commented or liked a comment stating, "You should write a book!" here you go, I did it. Thanks for the encouragement.

God, I will never completely understand your unconditional love for me until we are together. You gave me the perfect earthly Dad to walk it out in front of me. You gave me children to test my limits and prove to me the needle never moves in my amount of love for them, no matter what. You gave me countless spiritual mentors, night skies filled with northern lights, your soft gentle voice, and your unwavering standard of holiness. I've fallen short in so many ways and still don't know how to reconcile all of that, but I know you're true, you're faithful, and you're the never-ending fountain of hope in my soul without whom I would not have made it this far. For whatever time you have appointed for me, let me be strong, let me be soft, let me be courageous, and let me be true with your message. ~Amen

INTRODUCTION

MY HELLO

SOUTH DAKOTA FARMER'S DAUGHTER. UNWILLING LUCILLE BALL MOMENT SURVIVOR. REJECTION-SENSITIVE OVERCOMER. LOVER OF LIFE. SEEKER OF JOY.
I am the perfect storm of my parents. I have the Lucille Ball gene from my mom. If there's something awkward to be said, it'll be flying out of my mouth at the most inopportune times. If there's a least graceful moment to trip over my own two feet and land flat on my face or have a wardrobe malfunction, it'll happen to me automatically. Like my dad, when these things would happen to my mom or anyone else, my first instinct is to laugh until I cry. If someone gets hurt (but they're okay), I'll help them, but they're going to have to give me a second to stop laughing first. I know how to love hard and lift others up to be the best they can be. Stubbornness and determination were poured into me in double portions. I am the perfect storm of the Nuttall and Bush families.

I spent most of my life practicing self-rejection religiously, maybe even more consistently than my faith. With every successive birthday, I started taking a longer look at who

I was and how I'd gotten here to be fifty. I think that's a normal thing.

In a Netflix documentary about his life, *The Last Dance*, Michael Jordan said, "As you get older, you look back and you understand how you became the person you are." I had already begun this review of my life, and what I found was pretty fascinating, at least to me.

I used to spend a significant part of my life rejecting myself, being embarrassed of myself, and trying to hide my imperfections. I often played the defensive role in life while doing damage control and wondered why it wasn't working. The older I became, the more I was able to own my Lucille Ball Moments. I shared them with friends and even started posting them on my social media pages. I became the person people could laugh at—only this time, it wasn't embarrassing. I could honestly see the humor in all these moments and knew that if I were on the outside, it would bring me great joy to witness the chaos as well. So, I took it all in, and here we are.

As I interviewed people for this book, I noticed a theme. People fell into one of a few groups.

- ***The Defensive Line:*** Many people were sitting back playing defense with their life.
  - They felt the peace between the gut punches were enough. They were letting life direct them instead of proactively causing their life to travel a certain way. Life is totally in control for them; they just wait to see what it brings next. This used to be me.

- ***Special Teams Standouts:*** This group viewed age with a little trepidation, mostly directed toward what health issues might arise for them or their loved ones.

- "I'm afraid I'm going to have lived this incredibly beautiful life and not be able to remember any of it!" she said as she pondered her possible future. Alzheimer's ran in her family, and she had to consider the possibility.
- "All I want before I die is a minute of peace," she sighed after recounting all that she's experienced as an registered nurse in health care.

- *The Replay Officials*: A gentleman who describes himself as a negative person said, "We should want to make a difference in this world, but I'm glad I'm closer to the exit door than the entrance door." He also stated fear that he hadn't done enough of the right things all his life.

- *The Quarterback Club:* The last group, and the one I now so deeply identify with, are the ones who don't play defense. We are offense, and we are calling the plays every day without letting one day just roll into the next.
  - "I don't want to look back and think, 'I wish I would've . . .'" This amazing teacher has a specific plan for the things she is going to accomplish. I get her.
  - "I feel like I've lived a life carrying an umbrella of fear because of some things that happened early on. Right now, I'm being intentional about folding up that umbrella and putting it away." She wants to own her own hydroponics business as soon as she retires from her first career in nursing. Again, she speaks my language.

The people in The Quarterback Club are the kind who are always looking for something to make the moment

MY HELLO · 13

memorable. It doesn't necessarily mean that things are easy for these adventurous, grab-life-by-the-horns people, it's just who they are. I recently went back to South Dakota, and while running an errand with a friend, they just ran right off the road on purpose and drove out into the middle of a cornfield so we could check the corn. Of course, that's not something you could do all the time, but spontaneity is a great companion for those of us looking to make every moment count. These are my people. We have the same drive to get to where we want to be.

I am in the second half of my life, and I've started a new career as an author. Although I still have one child at home, I'm now able to do something for myself, and writing this book is my great adventure. For the first half of my adult life, I wholeheartedly wanted to be and gave myself to being a wife and mom—to pour into those whom I loved the most and help them become successful. I wasn't perfect, but I did what I could, and when I learned better, I did better. I'm not fond of my mistakes, but I refuse to dwell on them. I realized over the years that this is who I am; the whole package is beautiful and should be celebrated. I think sharing my triumphs and blunders equally relieves the pressure of living up to everyone's social media perfection standards. I'm being much more intentional about connecting with people and giving them some joy in their day. You have to look for the funny to have joy.

After living with so many awkward moments I couldn't control, I affectionately dubbed them my Lucille Ball Moments. Trying my hand at cussing was probably the first disaster I could identify as the beginning of a career unwillingly creating these shenanigans. They just kept coming, and eventually, I embraced them as part of who I am.

After hearing my mom describe what one of my brothers was like as a baby recently, I asked her, "What was I like as a baby? In all my years, I don't think I've ever heard you describe me." I wanted to see if there was anything left of the kid I remember before "life" set in.

She said, "I would describe you as a baby the same way I would describe you today. You entered this life on the go, and there wasn't any adventure you weren't up for. You never played with toys because your joy came from talking to and connecting with whatever person was around. You walked at seven months and talked full sentences at twelve months. There was no stopping you after that."

That feels right. I think the part of me that desired to connect with people has been the same since birth. Today I would rather meet someone new and hear their story than go shopping or most other activities.

As I started to write, it was almost like I was charting a timeline for when major negative events invaded my happiness. It became easier to see what challenges or character flaws sprouted up in my life like suffocating weeds after each event. I never doubted myself when I was little. I was a boss, confidence for days, and overall, a very optimistic kid. That didn't last long.

As I began to think about how many people I knew who struggled with the effects of rejection, I also knew how many new rejection-sensitive hearts were being born every day. I wanted to reach out with my story to let them all know they aren't alone and there is hope.

From the time I felt like cussing at my dad would make us great friends (horrible decision, really), to overcoming the "I Hate Heather Nuttall Club" in middle school, walking through a decade of my husband's addiction, all of it was hard, but not everything was awful. There have been many, many moments of love, fun, and ridiculousness along the way thanks to embracing my Lucille Ball Moments (oof that took a minute!). From making my husband give me a Brazilian bikini wax (do I really need to say what kind of decision that was?) to the moment he cut off every single one of my eyelashes (really horrible, no good, rotten decision on his part), I hope my story brings many moments of laughter and a brighter outlook on embracing your whole self and beginning to attack life in all the ways that leave you breathless with hope.

Blessings y'all . . . we need 'em every day!
Heather

CHAPTER 1

CUSSING ISN'T ALWAYS THE COOLEST

———

I was always told by the world that you couldn't use words like "ass" and be a Christian. Really, you couldn't use words like that and be a classy, responsible adult if you wanted to get right down to it. Over time, curse words—including the dreaded "F" word—became part of the normal vocabulary in music, writing, television, backyard barbeques, and coffee at the kitchen table. So many people made it a regular part of life, yet I knew they were responsible, classy, and genuinely good people who also loved God. I had to reevaluate what I knew. It caused me to go back and remember my first event with swearing at someone. I tried my hand using swear words for the first time on my dad. Goodness, that was a bad decision.

I love my dad bigger than big. So many of my life's values come from watching him and mimicking him in my own way. We were farmers and ranchers in a tiny town in rural South Dakota. I watched the way my dad stood, the way he carried himself, how he handled himself in conversations with peers, and I took it all to heart. Many times, another farmer would come over to buy or trade an animal, sell us some goods, or see how the crops and family were doing. I was always underfoot and heard many of these conversations.

My dad never really cussed. Maybe "hell" was the closest thing I remember him saying often enough to be considered a habit. But many other farmers let the blue words fly, and my dad really enjoyed their company. Making him happy was something I craved. I wanted to stand around and have conversations with him and make him laugh the way they could. I now understand this to be the difference between adult friendships and the company of children. Your reactions and level of friendship aren't the same, but you couldn't convince me of that when I was six!

Before we go any further, let me remind you that as I am telling these stories and these vivid memories from my childhood, you're hearing them from the perception of a five- or six-year-old. Places, events, the sizes of people and buildings should be filtered through the knowledge that you're hearing what a child remembers. While researching these events through conversations with my family, I learned just how off a young child's memory could be. For authenticity's sake, I'm going to tell them just as my little heart remembers, regardless of the errors.

One time, the Watkins man came by trying to sell whatever his special was that month. Watkins' products ranged from pure baking vanilla to dishwasher soap, if I remember correctly. It's fun to still see Watkins vanilla in Walmart and to this day, it's what I buy, remembering poor Wendell every time. This visit proved to be profoundly disastrous and initiated my little ears to the fact that there was more than "hell" and "damn" as cussing options.

I had finally gotten my very own billy goat as a pet a few months before. He roamed free, or maybe he just had gotten out that day, but that's not the point. When the Watkins man pulled up in his fancy Cadillac, my billy was nowhere to be found. Hellos and pleasantries were exchanged, and we went in the house to see what samples the Watkins man brought us this time. While we were inside, Billy hopped up on the Cadillac and must have done the fanciest little tap dance ever seen—from the hood to the trunk. It must have been the happiest he'd ever been in his whole life because from the hoof marks and scratches, it was obvious he had pranced up and down that car multiple times. I wished I could have seen his little face while he was doing it because I was sure it would have been precious.

Precious, however, was not the word the Watkins man used—repeatedly. Dad sent us all into the house and dealt with him alone to protect our innocent ears. This poor man just about had a stroke before leaving our farm that day. I kind of felt like he had grossly overreacted.

Later while Dad was having coffee with one of his brothers and a few friends, I overheard him telling the story and laughing so hard his face was beet-red describing how upset the Watkins man was. He was repeating all the words that ol' boy kept yelling while flailing his arms toward my billy goat. Everyone laughed, especially my dad. I wanted to be like that with dad. I wanted to tell stories back and forth and laugh together.

I had been pondering for a while how I would do it. How I would use my first cuss word and make Dad laugh, thus ushering me into the realm of being his peer and friend? Does anyone else feel a sense of foreboding at this very moment? If this were a movie, the soundtrack would be building suspense through music right now.

The night finally came. It was my turn to take the trash out to the burn barrel and watch it burn so it didn't start any grass fires. I was a bit young, maybe six or seven, so I didn't ever really get to do this chore without a chaperone. Dad was my chaperone and companion this night while the trash was burning. I was wearing my best bell-bottom jeans, a tight belly-showing shirt, and with my pixie haircut, I had all kinds of confidence. I was feeling like the rite of passage was knocking with opportunity. I noticed our orange tomcat in the tree line, and he appeared to be just staring at us for an unreasonably long amount of time. I remember adjusting my stance with one foot slightly in front of the other, slipping my thumbs into my belt loops like I had seen the old farmers do, and lifting my chin ever so slightly to nod in the tomcat's direction.

"What's that son of a bitch staring at?"

I did it! I said a cuss word, just like all the old farmers. I had thought everything out and couldn't wait to see my dad's laughter, complete with the mischievous sparkle in his eye that I loved so much and the laughter lines. I turned my face up to see him and well, the mood couldn't have changed any faster had someone just dropped a snake down my shirt, let's just say that. Dad did not have a twinkle in his eye. In fact, his eyes narrowed, and I was pretty sure I saw tiny little flames leaping out of them. I vividly remember two physical responses to this moment. Immediately after I saw his face, I remember feeling my face fall. My little face had been all upturned into a smile, awaiting the sound of laughter from my dad. When my eyes met his, I think I remember feeling my cheeks bounce a little because my face fell so fast. I was in complete shock, and my mouth was hanging wide open.

The second physical response I felt also had to do with cheeks, but not the ones on my face. Did you ever do something as a child and just immediately know you were going to get a whoopin'? Y'all, the rate of speed and the power of the butt pucker that happened the moment my eyes met his were of historical, epic proportions.

The experts say you have two responses to stressful situations: fight or flight. The experts are wrong. I had neither. If at any moment in my little life, I would have enabled the go-ahead for flight, it would have been to flee straight to my dad. He was my safety and my stability. Everything bad could be stopped just by being near my dad. In this case, however, that did not appear to be the wisest of decisions, and I'd just made a decision worse than Wile E. Coyote did every Saturday when he rigged up explosives to trap the Road Runner. I decided to just stand still, waiting for whatever was to come. Discipline might not have been fun, but he could always be trusted, so I waited.

The other option: fight. Like many of the kids who grew up in the seventies, you might be ready, willing, and able to fight for yourself anytime, anyplace, or anywhere, but fighting your parent was just a whole other universe and one you did not consider. Not with your mouth or your body.

So there I stood, in all my butt-puckered, jaw-dropping glory. I heard the familiar clicking sound my dad would make with his mouth sometimes, and then I heard him say.

"Young lady, what did you just say to me?"

Well now, why did he have to do that? Clearly, we both understood that the tomcat sentence was a very regrettable decision. Now he wanted me to repeat it? I opened my mouth to say it again, although I thought maybe Dad was making a very regrettable decision himself, but when I went to speak, there appeared to be a giant stone planted straight in the center of my throat.

"Those words you used are not the words we use in this family. We know a lot of people who talk like that. We enjoy them as people, we laugh with them, we share a meal with them, and we love them, but we don't talk like them. They can use whatever words they want because they are adults. It's not our place to tell them they are wrong. But as a family, we are not going to use those words. You are the prettiest little thing ever, and I don't want to ever hear ugly words like that coming out of your mouth, making the moment ugly again. Do you understand?"

"Yes sir," I said.

And then, to drive home the lesson, I submitted to the discipline necessary to receive that extra little reminder. It's not accepted to discipline kids today the way I got it. They say no matter how it's done, a "whoopin'" is always abuse. I never felt abused. It was always right across my rear end—except for the one time I got slapped for backtalking with disrespect. I deserved that too. I was pushing the limit to see how ugly I could treat my mom when I was getting just a little too high and mighty.

Dad used a belt; my mom sometimes used her hand or a flyswatter. I did learn from my parents and those whoopin's. Did I like getting a spanking? No child likes it. Did I learn the lesson after the first round of discipline for certain behaviors? No, most certainly not. Like I said in the introduction, stubbornness and determination were poured into me with double portions. Sometimes that "woodshed" had a significant path worn to it. Was it the only form of discipline they used? No, it was a last resort, but that didn't mean certain events couldn't just catapult you right past all the other options and land yourself on "You're getting a whoopin' right now." Using the phrase "son of a bitch" with your dad was a "Do Not Pass Go—Do Not Collect $200" kind of moment.

As always, after discipline, my dad and I were restored. I got the punishment, we talked about it, he held me and hugged me, we finished burning the trash and laughed together. Thank goodness that dumb cat was long gone. I really didn't like him very much anymore.

It was the first time I realized that sometimes things are lawful for some people, but not always for everyone. Sometimes I get to do something that other people don't have the freedom to do for whatever reason, and vice versa.

One of my daughters can use the "F" word in every grammatical scenario imaginable. She didn't learn this in my home. After my burn barrel experience, cussing hasn't ever really become comfortable for me, and certainly not that word. She can make it a noun, a verb, an adverb, a dangling participle . . . well you get the picture. It makes me cringe every time I hear her or anyone else use it. It also makes me a bit sad thinking about "making the moment ugly" as my dad put it. Out of respect, she tries to catch herself and not use it around me much, but if I ever try to throw out words like that, I am once again standing in front of the burn barrel in my little red Keds with my pixie cut and my belly hanging out, butt puckered and feeling very much exposed.

CHAPTER 2

JUST WHAT IS A LUCILLE BALL MOMENT ANYWAY

If you're a Lucille Ball fan, you likely have seen the episode or short video clips of Lucy in the chocolate factory with her friend Ethel. They're too scared of the supervisor, or maybe they are just too proud to admit they can't keep up with wrapping the little chocolates as they come down the conveyor belt, and they tell her this is no problem! The supervisor then yells to the assembly line to speed it up. You can immediately see the worry and the panic on Lucy's face as she knows she's going to get caught in a lie. She begins to shove those candies in her pockets, in her shirt, and in her hat. All to no avail, and she gets caught anyway, which results in her getting fired.

These are the moments I find myself in. For some reason, when things start to spiral out of control, like Lucy, I'm apparently incapable of choosing the words or actions that would actually help. If she would've just told the supervisor that she couldn't keep up and needed a little more time at the slower pace, maybe it would've turned out differently.

Internally, I panic. While in panic mode apparently, I'm just not able to pick the word or action to smooth everything out. Nope, I choose the most awkward thing and ride that mistake until everything blows sky high.

Then there are the lesser Lucille Ball Moments, the times when I'm out in public only to find that my shirt is on inside-out. You would think it couldn't have happened that often, but you'd be wrong; it's happened so many times that I just shrug my shoulders and carry on. If it's backward, I have no problem just swinging it around right there in front of God and everyone.

Sometimes, there are innocent bystanders who become victims of my moments. Not too long ago, I needed to buy a piñata for a birthday party. I had my thirteen-year-old daughter with me. Things would've been fine if I would've just gone with the cute ones down low that we could reach. But before we left the aisle, I noticed, way above the shelf dangling from a hook was an even cuter piñata. It was the only one of its kind, and for sure it was way out of reach. But I wanted it!

First, I tried the whole short-girl thing and tried to climb up the shelves a little to see if I could reach it. I could barely touch the bottom, but I couldn't get it lifted over the hook. Since I'm a short girl who also likes to eat, I was a little hesitant to try and climb up to the next shelf. Hmmm Plan B . . . that's when I look over and see my daughter.

I tried to coerce my thirteen year old (who is daughter number five) to climb into the cart and I would push her next to the shelves where she could kind of rock wall climb up to get the elusive piñata. That was a no-go for her. Since birth, she has struggled with a balance disorder that leaves her dizzy most of the time, and she thought that this might possibly be the worst thing I'd ever suggested in her life, considering the struggles.

Not one to give up easily, I convinced her that if she would climb into the Walmart shopping cart and then onto my shoulders, I would be able to have balance for both of us and we could obtain this dang piñata. She reluctantly agreed. She made it onto my shoulders easy enough. I turned around and headed for the piñata on the upper deck. But as she was reaching for the piñata, she also reached out to steady herself with her other hand. Whatever it was that she grabbed moved and fell all the way to the ground. This caused her to lose her balance and jerk real hard. Her jerking real hard was not something my mind had accounted for. She jerked one way, I twisted the other way, and my knees buckled. We went down hard.

Half of everything on the shelves was now down around my feet, and I'm positive at this point we are going to get caught. In the birthday aisle there are all of the grab bag goodies for the parties; tiny little birthday army men, fancy plastic rings, and noisemakers were scattered all over the floor. I'm crawling all over on my hands and knees, frantically trying to pick up merchandise to throw it haphazardly back onto the shelves when another customer tentatively peeked around the corner. He was a giant of a man, and after hearing the commotion, he appeared in our aisle with a smirk on his face. My daughter is red-faced and would rather hide under any of the nearby shelves, but we had already been caught. I instantly crawled back up to a standing position, hoping the awkwardness of his first vision of me crawling around on all fours scooping things up to throw back up on the shelves could somehow be erased. By the smirk on his face and the chuckle just below the surface, I could tell it had not worked.

Having a lifetime of Lucille Ball Moments, I just giggled and shrugged my shoulders. I asked him if he could reach the piñata and put me out of my misery. I heard my daughter groan with embarrassment behind me. He grinned and reached for it, pulling it down on the first try. Then I asked him if he could also forget all interactions with us on this day and never tell a soul what he had seen. He very gentlemanly agreed to do that for me, and with a tip of his hat, he walked around the corner still getting a giggle over the lady crawling on all fours he had just encountered in the birthday aisle.

Problem solved, and I was feeling pretty good about myself, even though there were still dozens of things we had knocked off the shelves all around our feet. One look at my daughter reminded me that she had not had a lifetime of Lucille Ball Moments and she was very much disgusted with what I'd just put her through. We're still working on her tolerance for these moments; it's a process of repeated exposure and living through it.

On a different occasion, with a different daughter (my second daughter). I was bringing her to school in the morning. She was a freshman in high school. She attended a private Christian school in another nearby town. It was a little bit of a novelty because Garth Brooks' daughter attended the same school. He and Trisha are super sweet and down-to-earth people, normal by all descriptions. Not to my daughter: she revered them as the superstars they are and felt like they should be treated with the utmost care and respect.

While dropping her off at school, I had to pull in under a carport. It went from very sunny, the kind of morning sunshine that's almost blinding, to a super shaded area, and going from one extreme to another was a little difficult to adjust to. My daughter was probably fourteen at the time, filled with angst that she had to be connected to such embarrassing creatures as parents, double portions of sass and rebellion; and pretty much just looked forward to the time when she could get out of the car each morning and put some distance between her and her embarrassing mom.

As I pulled in under the carport, I couldn't see anything because of the drastic change in sunlight. To my left were the doors of the elementary school. I could see children on the sidewalk by the well-lit doors and had focused all my attention on them to avoid hitting one of them. All of a sudden, someone slapped my hood forcefully and yelled, "Hey!"

I'm trying to figure out where this man came from. He was standing directly in front of my car and clearly, I had missed him trying to cross in front of me because I was watching the kiddos on my left. My daughter groans, "Oh My Gosh!" and hit the floorboards. I'm looking at her down on the floor and back up at this man who almost dented the hood of my car when it dawns on me: It's Garth Brooks. I literally almost ran over Garth Brooks. He was dressed in a black jacket and had on a black baseball cap. Remember how I said that it was really dark under the carport when you left the sunlight? Well, it would have been really helpful if he hadn't been wearing black, but he didn't ask my opinion when he got dressed that morning, so there we were, staring at each other through my windshield. My eyes were huge, my face was turning red, my daughter was on the floorboards of the car whisper yelling at me, "You are so embarrassing! You almost ran over Garth freaking Brooks! I'm not going to school today, just turn around and take me home because I'm not getting off the floorboards of this car!" Still maintaining eye contact with Garth while my child was in teenage hysterics, I did what I know how to do: I laughed, hard.

He instantly pointed at me and smiled his big award-winning smile and yelled, "Have a great day!" and scooted on through the carport and into the elementary wing. The fact that I quickly rolled down my window to shout, "Oh my word, I am so sorry!" to his retreating backside prompted yet another round of hissing from the floorboards, but it was the polite southern thing to do after almost running over someone.

To this day, that daughter won't let me live down the fact that I almost robbed the world of the gift that is "Garth freaking Brooks!" He lived, we lived. It's fine, I'm fine, he's fine, everything's fine! Except my daughter maybe.

After all my Lucille Ball Moments, it's amazing that my daughters still are willing to go places with me! Two summers ago, another daughter (number four) and I went to Boston, Massachusetts, so we could attend a couple of Boston Red Sox games together. We toured all of Boston, met the sweetest old Italian Uber driver who talked and sounded exactly like Rocky Balboa, ate at Legal Seafood, and attended two games two days in a row.

On my first embarrassing event, while eating at Legal Seafood, we had to sit at the bar because there was no room anywhere else. There was an older, fancy-looking couple on our right—fancy in the sense that she looked a little like what Jacqueline Kennedy Onassis would probably have looked like at this age and both of their white heads of hair appeared to shine like icicles you would hang from your Christmas tree. We ordered pork rinds and crab dip as an appetizer because all the other seafood items just seemed a little bit too . . . well . . . seafood-ish for us. When the appetizer came, it solidified my belief in the fact that I do not like pork rinds, and the crab dip was warm. We were less than enthused. We offered it to the older couple, as we had just begun to strike up a conversation with them.

"Do you not like it?" the woman asked.

Me: "Not so much. I'm sure it's wonderful, it's just that well, (*I pause*) we're from Oklahoma and pretty much we just eat red meat and potatoes (*I shrug my shoulders*)."

Him: "Tell me exactly what you don't like."

My daughter: "Well, I'm not sure that I like warm crab dip. I was expecting cold, and it just was kind of a turn-off."

Me: "The pork rinds seem a little chewy, but I'm a little iffy on pork rinds anyway so who knows."

The man reached over and took one of the pork rinds and popped it in his mouth. At this point, I could see the bartenders are acting a little uneasy. One might think that I would have begun to catch on here, but I did not. Shortly after our meal, which I'm thankful we both loved and gave happy compliments about to our new friends, a plate of delectable little chocolate desserts showed up. The couple each took one and passed the plate to us with one for each of us.

Her: "I hope you like these!"

Me: "Are these your favorites?"

Her: "It's my recipe."

Me: ". . . (*My mouth gapes open. I have to force myself to close it again.*) . . . your recipe . . ."

Him: "Yes, my wife and I founded Legal Seafood fifty-two years ago, and we've been married for fifty-five years." He looks so proud of his bride and all that they had accomplished that his shirt buttons might as well have popped.

Me: "Oh my goodness, I am so sorry about every word that came out of my mouth this evening. I really had no experience with which I could judge seafood, and I'm so sorry that I even ventured to. (*Face-palm*)"

At this point, my daughter's mouth had slammed shut and her eyes were the biggest I'd seen since she flooded the entire upstairs of our house as a child. We were both literally sitting there feeling like we would never be able to remove our feet from our mouths. Instead, they were wonderful and gracious. They paid for our appetizer and our dessert, gave us some life and marriage advice, and let us take a picture with them. He said that to be successful you have to be forgiving to others, but mostly to yourself. He also added, "Don't try to be great at everything; excel at one thing and the rest will come. You have to work hard and love hard, but in the end, you're going to need just a little of one more thing: luck. Everyone needs a little bit of luck along the way."

It was a wonderful accidental meeting, but seriously, I had just told this man his pork rinds were chewy and didn't really measure up to Oklahoma's red meat and potatoes. Might as well insert Gomer Pyle's dorky laugh here because it couldn't have been more ridiculous.

We headed to the game, riding the subway and navigating our way through the streets to Fenway. I was wearing cropped blue jeans with a really cute pink button-down shirt and a cross-body purse. My daughter was also in jeans and was wearing a T-shirt with a knot tied in the back; she was of course looking as cute as her twenty-three-year-old self could look. While making our way toward the stadium, we crossed the David Ortiz Bridge.

David Ortiz, or Big Papi as he was affectionately called was literally who made me like the Red Sox, and I decided that we needed a picture with the sign. The street in front of us was packed with traffic and they were at a standstill. As we were struggling to get a perfect selfie with the sign in the background, a van full of men laughing boisterously called to us and said we were looking exceptionally beautiful. They volunteered to take a picture for us so we could get all of the sign in the background. I figured what could the harm be, right? They weren't going anywhere anytime soon, and we could certainly use some help with this picture.

I run out to the end of the sidewalk, lean over, and hand my phone to the man in the passenger seat. Now listen, the size of the grins across the faces of these men should have immediately caused me to stand up and take inventory of myself. But Italian men can be boisterous, they can be all about the moment, and I was all about getting this picture. As I'm handing off the phone, one of the men says, "Mama, you're looking exceptionally fine tonight!" I flippantly said, "Thank you!" and ran back to my daughter so they could snap the pic.

When they were done, I ran—God help me, I ran—back out to the street and retrieved my phone. Again, with the big grins and weirdly aggressive compliments. Not totally sure what I should do, I laughed with them, thanked them for taking the pictures, and teased them about being overly complimentary. I could hear their giggles as I walked away, and their car finally was able to inch forward down the street.

We made it into the stadium, found our seats, and passed roughly two million people on our way through the fan area. As we sat down, I pulled out my phone to look at the pictures. Y'all...

That crossbody purse I had? It had rubbed back and forth on my cute pink button-down shirt and had unbuttoned two large buttons, exposing my push-up bra and all that was being "pushed up" by the time I realized it was happening.

The top button had stayed buttoned; it was just the two large ones from there that betrayed me. There are four total buttons on the whole shirt. We had walked through the streets around Fenway, through the fan experience area, around the stadium inside looking for our seats, and I had been flashing my boobs at every dadgum person we walked by.

The pictures told the whole tale of why the van full of men thought I was looking "exceptionally fine" that night. I asked my daughter why she hadn't warned me.

"Mom, I'm at Fenway for the first time in my whole life. I was so excited about everything that you're the last thing I was looking at today. I'm sorry!"

She wasn't embarrassed at all. In fact, she posted that picture, doctored up with an X in the right places (at least I hope she posted the one with the X) and a few of herself in Fenway on Snapchat. She tagged the ballpark. She posted her Venmo info and captioned it, "Who wants to buy ya girls a drink at the game tonight?" Remember the phrase, "If I'm lyin' I'm dyin'?" Well, she received over $400 that night from people at Fenway, people in Boston, and people from back home. I was shocked, embarrassed, and yes . . . proud of this kid of mine.

The next night it was confirmed that Lucille Ball Moments are in fact genetic when my daughter was grabbing her right butt cheek and said "Mama, did I sit in something wet? My rear end feels weird!" There it was: a giant hole in the seat of her shorts. Lucille Ball Moments are genetic. Poor kid. She walked around a good portion of that day holding her butt cheek to cover it up. Eventually, she got tired of that and just let it go. She's learning those Lucille Ball Moment survival skills: just let it go.

It is what it is. We can't get rid of these moments, so we live with them. I used to get so embarrassed when I was a kid or early adult and try to hide them from the world and make sure no one would laugh at me. But the more I lived it, the more I realized that the ridiculous things that happen to me are pretty funny—even I had to admit it. I finally embraced it and gave them a name. I started to share my misfortunes with all my friends. So many of them prompted responses from my friends such as, "You have to write a book and write all of these down! You make me laugh so much I search your name every time I log in to social media!"

One day, a lady introduced herself to me in a restaurant and told me that sometimes, my being honest about my embarrassing and awful moments as much as my life successes was the only thing that kept her going some days.

If I really can do that for someone, I will share them every single time.

It brings me joy to bring joy to others. There's nothing I can do to avoid these events, so we all might as well have a giggle together.

CHAPTER 3

SANDS THROUGH THE HOURGLASS

My first experience with a "midlife crisis," or panic attack at the thought of growing older, was not with myself. It was with my husband when he was twenty-nine! (Insert eye-roll here). The thought of turning thirty bothered him so much he was in a full-blown state of dreading the upcoming birthday the entire year... When he did turn thirty, he spent that whole year upset and grumpy because he was now "old" (Insert even harder eye roll here). I told myself then that I would never let life do to me what it did to him regarding age.

He wouldn't have described himself that way, but we noticed every harsh remark when he previously would have joked with us. What I saw happening was a good man gaining ground in his career and financially stepping up to a new level. Instead, all the while, he was becoming very moody, and his optimism disappeared more every day that went by.

He had gone almost a decade without drinking anything. Now he is in the woodworking shop, drinking and trying to hide any evidence that he was doing so, even lying about it. I tried to make myself clear that I didn't care about the drinking, but him hiding it and lying was where we would fight every time.

There were things me or the girls could do that would produce a negative reaction in him we would have never expected. While he was caught up in the process of having to deal with all the things happening to him internally, I was left to deal with all that those feelings produced in his life, and it wasn't fun.

In his thirtieth year, we moved into a custom-built home on a quiet cul-de-sac in a neighborhood he'd had his eye on since we had moved to town. At this point, we had four daughters, and the two oldest girls were getting close to middle school with all sorts of activities creeping in to steal any downtime we would have had as a family. We didn't really get a break to just be together where a healthy conversation could have occurred and maybe relieve some of his stress. Therefore, I was not any help to him.

Not only was I not any help, but my little German temper could only hold off for so long before I reacted strongly to him snipping at me or the girls for some random inconvenience that just hit him wrong. We were establishing a pretty unhealthy routine of dealing with each other's moods while rushing kids back and forth to school functions and little league sports.

We went through a test of fire from our thirties to our forties, and my ability to see positivity or hope was in danger of being extinguished. He went through a decade that started with the worry and depression of turning thirty, then the loss of his father which really hit him hard, and ultimately an addiction that just about tore our family apart and ruined us spiritually, personally, and financially. Life doubled down with hits to our finances when we lost 30 percent of our wages and benefits after the 9/11 terrorist attacks. His frustration with life lead to insomnia, which led to a doctor visit, which led to him being prescribed Ambien. Some people tout Ambien as a miracle cure for their problems. It was the beginning of a nightmare for us. It set up an almost decade of addiction that assaulted him. Some people asked me why I stayed for a decade. I'm not going to go into all the details about the ways this drug tried to ruin our lives and the actions he committed during this time. But one of the things that kept going through my mind was that he didn't start drinking excessively or knocking down pills from a lifestyle of hanging out with "the guys" or running the town. This happened when he reached out for help from a professional. He was inadvertently being assaulted by a drug he tried through complete trust in the medical community. He told me once, "Ambien is the strongest drug I have ever taken, and with the first one I knew I was in big trouble."

During this decade, my emotions were all over the place. Ambien causes amnesia of events with some people, and for sure it did with my husband. I never knew whether he would remember all the things he was supposed to do for our kids while I was running the other ones to their events. He never remembered that I had told him what needed done. I would shout that I had told him, and at that point, one of the kids might as well have rung the bell for Round 1 in a WBA heavyweight boxing match because it . . . was . . . on! I developed a habit of nagging all the time, thinking at some point the part of him that could remember would finally cause him to get the girls to their games or practices. Of course, men hate being nagged, and the vicious cycle just repeated itself.

I developed clinical depression, restless leg syndrome, fibromyalgia, degenerative disc disease, and a few other cute little diagnoses during this time. I was propelled forward by the desire to make sure my kids lacked for nothing. One of us always had to be at all their practices, games, and school functions. My parents were always there for all my events, and it was a comforting, special feeling for me; I wanted my kids to have the same. It was something that drove me. Plus, it kept me from having to stay at home and get on the merry-go-round of emotions with my husband again.

By the time he came out of it and was on solid ground again, I was starting to find myself. I was forty-four, and now that I only had one young child at home, life was a lot less chaotic. I had a hysterectomy that year, and even though it sent me into full-blown menopause, I felt strong in body and young in spirit. Most of our older children were graduating high school or college, and it was just a fun time.

By nature, we are total opposites (how cliche right?). He is a total pessimist, and I'm forever the optimist, seeing hope in all situations. He lives to die someday, and I'm dying to live every day. We annoy each other in these terms. I've loved him since I was a teenager, and we've been best friends since we were around thirteen years old.

My sense of humor is to poke fun at myself and all the things I've lived through. He is my other half and therefore gets poked fun at right alongside me because he's my partner in life. He has given me the green light in describing our life this way, so almost every story with the two of us in it will be poking fun at us in some way or another.

Around forty-eight years old, I began to take notice of all the stuff in my world. Life just did its thing and didn't care what my opinion was about that, not one bit! Time raced by, wrinkles appeared, I had to grunt getting up off the floor, and my sleep habits were all messed up. I had gained weight and was now surviving at the weight that I had always climbed to by the time I was nine months pregnant with my babies. (What!) I had so many medical diagnoses that had piled up over the years I carried medicine around by the duffle bag.

I began to take stock of myself. Who was I? I knew that I was a daughter, sister, wife, lover, mother, and even a granny, but who was I? How did I become the girl that always looked people in the eye? Why was I so much more willing than others to take a chance? How was I the lady who lived through one embarrassing Lucille Ball Moment after another? Where did the confidence go that I had when I would hold captive audiences at five years old and sing my heart out to them? It wasn't just the attention I loved, it was the song, the moment when others looked at each other and smiled, it was connecting the people to each other as they listened to me.

I know that I'm what others would call an "empath" today. I believe in God and try to slant my thoughts his way rather than the newest worldly terminology or fad the world at large is grasping onto, so I would have to say that I know I'm a person with mercy and discernment.

The empath part of me actually feels the emotions others are feeling. My husband can listen to a conversation and tell me later it was cool how they did this or that, but that's it for him. He lives in a world of logic and black and white. When I listen to someone, if they cry, my heart hurts and I cry. If I read a thread on Facebook where people are fighting and arguing, I feel the anger. I can look a woman in the eye and when I see joy in her soul, mine pounds with joy as well.

I can meet someone others have praised up and down, but from the first look into their eyes, my gut knows with very little error whether they are a genuine person or a danger in some way. If you know me well, you could read my first impression of someone when my eyes meet theirs. The older I've gotten, I've learned that I don't have to react every time I feel negativity or danger in someone. I didn't always handle it well when alarm bells went off regarding people, but all of that goes along with figuring out how to handle these gifts and traits.

People without this gift are just simply unable to understand how it works, how I can actually feel the emotions of others around me or things I read on social media. I am at a loss for how to explain it myself. All I can say is if you're close to someone who says these things, be patient with them. It's super confusing to see things and feel emotions from other people.

It takes a while to learn not to be driven to an emotional spin cycle all day long when sensing and feelings the emotions of others. It can be exhausting to be pulled back and forth by the empathy of feeling what others feel. We can be completely emotionally drained after a day working with others or even just being at a big happy family reunion. Any prolonged exposure to others whose emotions run high will undoubtedly affect us as well.

When you're tempted to say we are "moody," you are probably right, but until we learn how to navigate those things well enough to stay emotionally steady within ourselves, it's not really that we are moody. It's that we are carrying the moods of others and aren't quite sure how to shake it off. Be patient. At fifty, I've learned how to shoulder it for the most part. It comes, and we do eventually level out.

I saw a quote on social media that said, "A writer I think, is someone who pays attention to the world." I think this is true. I notice so many things going on around me at once and notice their emotions so clearly, it could leave other people dizzy.

I'm the lady who can be sitting at a restaurant in the Atlanta airport and notice a couple across from me who probably couldn't be more opposite of me if they tried: black leather jackets, more hardware pierced in them than my local hardware store carries, rings on every finger, and lime green hair. I don't kind of mean lime green hair, I mean bright, vibrant, almost looking for a light bulb under there somewhere lime green hair. I was fascinated. The actual color was stunningly beautiful. It was not a color I'd ever seen in hair before, but whatever! It. Was. Beautiful. I watched them banter back and forth with each other and really enjoyed my people-watching session. What did a couple like that talk about? Did they discuss the same things my girls did or were their conversations as eclectic as they appeared to be?

Before I had to leave to catch my flight, I decided that I would try and sneak a picture of her so I could show my girls. We were basically sitting across a countertop from each other. I could literally just act like I was sending a text and grab that pic.

But I have that Lucille Ball gene in me, as I've mentioned before, and when I went to sneak that picture . . . you guessed it: the flash was on. She pulled up short and looked me square in the eye and said "Was it good? Do you want a better one?" Normal people would be embarrassed, but I looked into her eyes and saw the twinkle. With a giggle, I replied "I just really love your hair. The color is super vibrant. I was trying to snap a pic to show my girls. Do you mind?" She grinned the biggest grin and struck a pose. She was delightful.

If I hadn't been observer, I wouldn't have seen the easy banter, the twinkle in her eye, and the gentle nature of her boyfriend. All I would've seen were the leather jackets, piercings, and weird hair. My husband and my mom would have straight up fainted for embarrassment at my situation and would probably have stolen my phone before I ever even attempted to snap that pic. But without that goof up, I would not have looked into the soul of someone with joy and gotten a really great picture of lime green hair. I was a little embarrassed for a minute, but I'm so glad I was paying attention.

I haven't always been good at navigating life. Sensing other people's emotions so strongly affected me deeply, and not knowing what to do with it left others confused or even hurt by all that goes on inside me. Throw in a couple of Lucille Ball Moments, and a German temper with my Gypsy bloodlines and you've got yourself one heck of a challenge that only the strongest and best can survive and love.

I didn't realize a pattern yet, but around that time I began to reevaluate all of the things in my life I ever thought I believed and began checking them off one by one.

CHAPTER 4

THE "I HATE HEATHER NUTTALL CLUB"

I'm not going to lie; this might be the hardest chapter that I ever write.

From middle school on, I've been the biggest, walking, breathing set of contradicting emotions ever documented. I am confident and yet the most insecure person you might ever meet. I am compassionate and aloof. I am loving, encouraging, and supportive to others, and yet I've believed and said the worst things to myself. I can get ready in the mirror and be pretty content with what I see until a picture is taken; then I see every flaw ever pointed out to me about myself all in a camera lens. I can see the strengths inside of other people without having a real conversation in some cases. I love calling that out in them and encouraging them to keep going. I love seeing hope in someone's eyes. At times I've tried to kill the very hope in myself.

How many times have we heard or said the phrase "Girls can be so mean!" They can. In my case, for one brief stint, they were all at the same time. Friends can really be the biggest blessing or the worst trauma in those formative years.

For me, girls were my nightmare and daydream all wrapped up into one. Living thirteen miles from town growing up, there were a lot of events and spontaneous get-togethers that I missed out on because it's just not that easy to drop everything and run to town when a last-second party starts up. Also, my parents were pretty immune to any guilt I tried to play to get them to take me to town every time I had a whim. I felt left out even though I understood why I was left out. It was kind of the same way with my birthday parties. Town girls all got along with me at school. I didn't really spend a lot of time fighting with anyone, but when I had a birthday party, there were usually only two girls who could find the time to come. Once or twice, I was invited to a birthday party in town, but it wasn't the norm. I never felt like I wasn't liked; there was always someone to play with at recess, and I never felt like anyone didn't want to sit by me in class. I didn't normally feel like I was the popular girl, but I felt like that title rotated from one girl to the next in our school. We had normal spats, and we recovered pretty quickly.

I know now that when others hurt me, it really doesn't tell the whole story of who they are inside. You can be a real jerk and a good person at the same time.

The following story is why I haven't written a book before, why I've always rejected myself, why I don't believe that deep down, anyone really, really loves me for who I am, why I always think I need to fit in their box to be loved, why love is only received when you perform. But also, I don't want to write this chapter because I also know that even in the moment, the actions of these girls severely betrayed the good that was in them. Today, I have wonderful relationships with most of them, and I don't want it to be viewed as bashing them in any way. But to completely tell my story, this one has to be in there.

Neither my mom nor I can remember exactly what grade it happened. But I'm sure it was middle school age—fifth or sixth grade probably. I honestly don't remember what happened to trigger this event. Was there a fight? Had I hurt someone? I don't know.

One day I got to school and literally every girl in my class simply would not speak to me. If I tried to say something, their smiles disappeared, and they would slowly turn their shoulders and walk away. That's it. I wasn't important enough of a living, breathing being for others to act like I even existed. There was one girl. She was one of my best friends, and she was a little more hesitant in treating me this way, but even she avoided conversation and contact with me. The other girl I considered a best friend participated as well even though it wasn't as ferociously carried out as some of the others. Same cold shoulder, same message delivered, and I heard it loud and clear: "You aren't worthy of oxygen. You are disgusting."

This isn't what they said verbally. It was the look, the slow roll of the shoulder, and the smirk as they turned their backs, refusing to acknowledge whatever I'd said. To me, it meant I wasn't worth living.

I don't even know how long this went on. If my heart were to judge, I'd say months and months. Okay, maybe it was weeks and weeks. My mom says she thinks it was a couple weeks. I don't know at all. It only went on long enough to split my soul. If that's ever happened to you, you understand. When your soul splits, it feels very detached. It's like everything you've ever known to be true is snatched from everything else in your brain. The two are coexisting inside of you, but like the food on my dinner plate, the two are not allowed to touch. Hope cannot exist with despair. Luckily for me, hope has yelled louder than despair for most of my life.

I attached myself to the boys in my class. Thank God they always scooted over and made room for me. They wouldn't talk about what was happening, but they didn't treat me the same way. They accepted me. I couldn't whine about what the girls were doing to me. I had to become one of the guys, and they didn't sit around whining about why people didn't like them. I went home and cried each night. Living so far out, I never got to go to town for frivolous things. I sat at home and cried and imagined all the fun, glorious parties they were having without me with and me being the center of hateful conversations. And I didn't know why . . . Maybe that was the torture. I didn't know why.

I instantly began to hate myself. Clearly, there was something in me to be rejected. All my friends since kindergarten were gone. I could see them, but they were gone.

Eventually, one of the girls approached me. To be honest, that was terrifying. Why? What was happening? Were they pulling me in just to make fun of me? Was she about to say something that would wound and haunt me forever? When she began to speak, I remember taking a deep breath. "Heather, I'm sorry for how we have acted. There is an 'I Hate Heather Nuttall Club,' and we were all in it. Everyone had to promise not to talk to you and not to be friends with you. I don't know if you can forgive me, but I left the club today. There was a journal and everything. We had to write down everything we hated about you. I'm sorry."

Whoa.

I will always remember where we were on the sidewalk when she told me. I mean, at least I knew, right? It should be over, right? As soon as the others found out I knew, the girls started defecting faster than roaches when the light turns on. Everyone told me so-and-so pressured them into it. It was a tight circle. There wasn't any one certain ringleader. They all blamed each other. It was someone else's idea. Everyone was "sorry."

If I remember correctly, there had been a sleepover after a birthday party. Some movie was watched where a similar club was created. I was one of the few not there. Bam . . . I became the headliner in the "I hate" club.

I got my hands on the journal somehow, and I devoured every word. One of the entries was about how they hated my freckles—in detail. My mom and dad loved those freckles. I used to feel special with them. Now I wanted to scrub them off.

I had really big front teeth. They weren't wrong. There was a big gap between them. They hated that so very much, and now I did too. I couldn't stand the reflection in the mirror.

They hated my favorite yellow shirt (rude!). I'm not backing down on this one. It was pretty. They can go suck eggs on that one.

They hated the way I played basketball.

They hated the way I laughed. The Nuttall laugh is loud and unique to each one of us, but you can tell that we are all related by that laugh. I love that, still do. They didn't steal that one from me. I have a daughter who has the Nuttall laugh. She is loud and proud with it. She is beautiful. She was voted "Best Laugh" as a senior in high school class of over 150 students. Oddly enough, that was super comforting for me. "Best" honors for something her mama had been persecuted for.

They hated that I had older brothers and it made me popular with the high schoolers. They hated my body. They hated that I had developed (really well). I was probably a C cup in fifth grade, and that never stopped. I was a DD before I left high school, and even after nursing babies, I landed at a DDD. Yeah, they can go suck eggs on that one too. I like my breasts. But no bragging on that. My mama would be on the phone with me the minute she got to this page if I did!

They named specific nights I'd been annoying. I probably was. I was in the awkward ten-to-eleven-years-old phase, and I didn't know who I was or what kind of person I wanted to be yet. I was testing the waters in everything.

I didn't know it yet, but I also needed glasses. Sometime in fifth grade, I got the beautiful late-seventies-early-eighties glasses frames and prescription lenses that took up a good one-third of the real estate on my face, but everyone else had them, so I felt awesome. I had a lot of weird going on. I'll admit it. But here's the deal: They were all the same age as me. One of them had big teeth too; another one had big glasses; one wasn't athletic; and one was just fussy all the time.

This experience made me judgmental. Toward others, yes, but the one I judged and passed the verdict of "unworthy" to daily was me. I couldn't look at myself in the mirror. That year, I started trying to change everything cosmetic they listed and a few more. There was no feature I had physically that I found to be okay. I instantly began to steal the little Ziploc bags of tiny rubber bands everyone wore on their braces. I would grab a package out of someone's locker or backpack. I wrapped four or five of those suckers around my top four teeth at night to pull them together. I would wear them almost every night. When I looked in the mirror, the gap between my teeth made me cry. Match that with those freckles and ugh, fountains of tears and self-loathing.

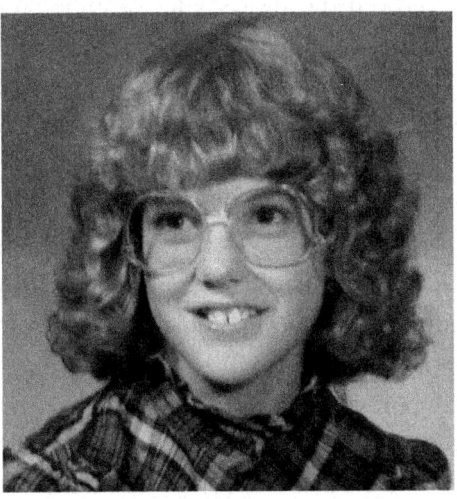

Ironically enough, my very first boyfriend had a gap between his teeth. He didn't hate it, and he didn't love it; it just was. I envied him so much. He represented a safe space for me. Maybe I desperately wanted him to teach me how to be okay with myself as much as he seemed to be. I wanted to be close to him to investigate this self-acceptance he had. It was intriguing and so attractive. It still makes me giggle today that I found him so attractive when he had the same trait that I tried desperately to rid myself of.

This guy was my first boyfriend and my first kiss. Apparently, I was his first kiss as well. I didn't know this until we were adults. But there we were at a movie party in someone's basement, slinking over to the darkest corner we could find, me with my front tooth gap I hated and him with his front tooth gap that was so attractive to me. I mean, if it was so attractive on Romeo, why couldn't I believe it was attractive on me? I digress. We were snuggled up together, he was whispering sweet nothings (I don't know what they were, but he always has been and always will be a smooth talker). The moment arrived. I knew it was coming; he stopped talking, looked me dead in the eye (I'm a sucker for eye contact), and he lowered his head. Everything was perfect and in slow motion. When at the point of no return, he came in hard—so hard he bumped teeth with me! Yep, you guessed it. He bumped my large, gapped front teeth! Well, one of them anyway. Come to think of it, one of them is a little darker than the other, no doubt from Romeo's excited, uncontrolled strong approach!

We were both embarrassed. He apologized and told me we should practice so we could get better, which I bought hook, line, and sinker. Even as adults, we have seen one another and teased each other about this. But this kissing failure was not my fault! In the eighties, the girls were not supposed to be super experienced, or we couldn't be "good girls." We had to depend on the guys to know what to do. Clearly, Romeo needed a little practice, and therefore, the embarrassing bumping of the teeth was not my fault. That's what I tell myself anyway whenever I get embarrassed by this memory.

That was a fun distraction from this wound and all it did to create me. I began to wear foundation makeup to cover my freckles; I made pretty good headway on my teeth, I even talked the dentist into filing them down when I was a junior so they weren't so big; and I did everything I could to make the girls like me again—everything.

This next part is awful for me to remember. I did everything to make them like me; when a month later they formed the "I Hate Brunelda Brown Club," I jumped in with both feet. Again, it happened because this girl wasn't there during a group sleepover. It wasn't that anyone hated her actually. There was a theme song, I sang it and clapped along—like the "Hercules, Hercules, Hercules!" clap. I was so all in, I might have even helped write the theme song. I actually liked Brunelda a lot. I was just unwilling to put myself in a situation where I would be the name that headlined the hate club ever again.

When my mom found out, she could not understand. "Heather, how could you? After everything those girls put you through?" I couldn't explain it. I just had to belong. Since nothing about me by itself was worthy of being loved, I just jumped in to do whatever it took to lessen the odds of ever being the headliner for the "I Hate …… Club" ever again.

I began to convince myself that no one ever really liked me. I began to lie uncontrollably. Whatever the person in front of me wanted to hear, that's the story I came up with. But of course, the next person wanted to hear other things, and before long, I got myself tangled up in such a nest that I couldn't iron out the truth from the lies. I had a moment my freshman year when I just had to throw my hands up at a party one night and say "Yep, I pretty much haven't told any of you the truth about anything in a very long time." They were all upset and didn't have much interest in speaking to me . . . again. I walked away from them and found a guy who was willing to make out for a while before I had to head home. That started a long, complicated square dance with the opposite sex. One of them was always willing, and I avoided hanging out consistently with girls again for the rest of high school. I would go through little spurts of activities with girls, and then I would find another guy.

My high school history teacher got a kick out of this. Every time he saw me flirting with someone new, he would yell "Nuttall!" and when I would turn around, he would be pretending to reel in a fish. By the time I was a junior in high school, when he would do this to me, I would reply with a snap of my fingers and a giant smile and say, "Next!"

I went from chasing one boy after another: date them, get them to say they loved me, love them back, and then break up with them at the first sign of them pulling away because the rejection of being broken up with was too much to bear. At any sign of a boy acting like he didn't think the sun and moon rose with my smile, they were gone. I was just broken. I feared the break-up too much to stick around and let it happen. Two of them surprised me and broke up with me before I could cut them loose, and it just piled on more and more self-loathing. It really, really is amazing that at the time of writing this book, I've been married for thirty-three years. You see, my husband has been pretty good at loving me himself, even with all the challenges and problems between us. He values me. It's not in the fairytale sense, but it's there, and it's really, really strong glue.

I have employed extreme measures. I have put myself down, isolated myself, hurt myself, and cut myself once to see if I could endure those things, look in the mirror, and genuinely feel sorry for who I saw inside. In the end, I opted for just avoiding myself: Stay busy, do only those things you're strong and good at, and never let anyone see your vulnerability.

About the time of my thirty-year high school reunion, I really began to break free from the feelings this trauma had created toward others. The girls who started the club? I have to remember they were also about eleven years old and understand all of the weirdness that brings out in girls. Through social media and reconnecting as the years went by, I knew what wonderful and genuine women most of them had become, and I just couldn't bring myself not to forgive them. We were eleven, they were just as unsteady in who they were as I was at that age, and I knew I couldn't hold a grudge with them. So many of them have great depths of compassion for others; they serve others without any hesitation and sacrifice for their families and communities. They did not mean to cause what happened to me. They did not know better, and I'd be darned if I was going to let that event rob me of wonderful nostalgic memories from as early as I could remember just because they were in them.

Back to turning fifty: I would say that I was about forty-eight when I really started to pick that hate club apart. It definitely played a huge part in how I dealt with my husband's addiction. I took it personally. It was rejection. Every time the fix was more important than the family, it screamed at me that we were unworthy, but mostly me. There was just no way I could be loved enough to help someone through addiction. I always fought this internal battle. I knew from the unconditional love my dad showed me that I was worthy somehow. Deep down inside, I knew I was loveable without needing to perform or become something someone else found valuable. I was valuable all on my own. I had begun to really grab ahold of unconditional love from God. I knew because of my dad's example what it felt like to be wholly accepted in the flesh and blood. Learning to accept the Lord's love was so much easier because of my dad's example.

I spent thirty years of my adulthood trying to get the woman who knew love to win the battle more than the one who felt she was unworthy of being loved. It's an internal battle worthy of fighting until you win. That's a hard thing to do sometimes, fighting "until."

Sometimes it would just be so much dang easier to give up and redirect my efforts onto something I felt was a strength and just try to compensate for my shortcomings in a different area. But avoidance doesn't bring peace.

Some battles are only meant for the "until."

Until you have victory. Sometimes, you step out there and do things to prove this to yourself, to gain victory, and in those actions, to hope to find a resolution. No one else may approve of or understand your attempts, but this is a personal hurt and trauma. Some call it Rejection Sensitivity Dysphoria. Like any other diagnosis, there is a huge spectrum. You can be the person no one suspects, or you can be highly reactive, aggressive, and depressed at the slightest form of perceived rejection.

I tried the other route—the push it down and deny it's a problem tactic—but it always came back. Luckily for me, the generational stamina to complete hard things comes from both sides, and I was always willing to engage in the battle again "until."

Until I gained control of myself and found my worth. I was way older than you would even suspect when I began to get ahold of this. My dad's example led me to the truth that God found me worthy just because. After I embraced that, I was able to find my worth in other things.

CHAPTER 5

THINGS MY PARENTS TAUGHT ME

I almost burned down the whole farm one time trying to destroy the evidence of what my friends and I had done over that particular weekend. My parents had left me at home alone because they trusted me. I deserved that whoopin' and the six weeks of grounding I got on top of it; I deserved it all. The only reprieve I got was prom, but not really. It just isn't the same experience when your mom delivers you to the gym and picks you up promptly at midnight (*sigh*).

My last whoopin' was when I was fifteen years old over that little stunt. Dad had ahold of my elbow, and I began running in circles, again with my butt puckered. He had his belt in his right hand; with his left hand, he had a firm hold on my left elbow. Out of dread and anticipation, I began to run in a circle. It was a circle because he had ahold of that elbow, and I wasn't getting out of his grasp. He ran right with me in those circles while walloping me three times on the rear end. On that day, I said that was probably the one

I deserved the most over my life, and even today I'll say it again: I deserved it.

Having to call the fire department to the farm because the corral was catching on fire and the barn would shortly be next . . . yeah, I deserved that one. Never once did I ever feel like my dad didn't love me unconditionally. Not all people are gifted enough to convey that to others, but he was.

My parents taught me that hard work determines the character of a man (or woman). I don't remember any times when my parents spent the whole weekend on the couch binge-watching anything. The times we did sit down for John Wayne, *Hee Haw*, Muhammad Ali, *The Wizard of Oz*, or *A Charlie Brown Christmas* Special were exactly that: special. Mom would always make popcorn or homemade chocolate malts, and the whole evening just became an event all its own.

My dad taught me to observe the people around me: people watching, he called it. Every time he was amused by something, he would raise an eyebrow at me and smirk while nodding in the direction of whatever mischief he had spotted, and we would share a silent laugh unless it was really funny, and then we were never able to hold it in.

My dad taught me to observe people and notice the humor in all things. Sometimes my mom would be the humor. Dad wasn't ever really making fun of her, but you see, the Lucille Ball Moments come directly from her. They are genetically passed down, and God love my girls, I've passed it on as well.

When I was in high school, I don't know why I could never remember which color basketball jersey we needed for each game. Actually, I do know why. The ADHD diagnosis came about twenty years too late, that's why. During one of my mom's first major Lucille Ball Moments, I remember being unable to control my laughter. She was making a mad dash to town to bring me the correct color jersey before the game started. It was cold, and I stayed just inside the lobby waiting to see her. She parked just a little to the south of the gym, and this caused her to have to take a different sidewalk than the straight, level one directly in front of the gym. I already had my basketball shoes on, and we weren't allowed to wear them outside, per my coach. I waited and watched her make her way toward the doors. In the last five feet, there was a small step down: just one. Bless her heart, she stepped off that curb and ended up flat on her face, arms and legs everywhere with my little jersey dangling at the end of one of her outstretched fists. She was so close to my double doors that I could only open them about four inches.

"Mom! Roll over so I can open the door and come help you!" I said through hysterical peels of loud Nuttall laughter. I tried to open the door to nudge her so I could squeeze out. It just pushed against her, and she moaned.

"Heather Marie stop that!" she shoved the jersey through the four inches of the open door and said, "Now get to the locker room and leave me alone!"

I could see several men rushing up the sidewalk to help her, and I knew she was going to be so frustrated that people saw her. I didn't feel right leaving her, but I couldn't get to her, so I just sat down on my side of the double doors, giggling while her frustrations grew.

Pretty much the same thing happened when we were in Pierre for a doctor's appointment one day. She took me to my favorite restaurant, Taco John's, for lunch. As we got close to the front doors, there was one step. Those one-step obstacles are just a little tricky for her, I guess. I stepped up and went to open the door for her when I heard "Oh!" followed by a thud. I ran back to her calling her name, but I couldn't help her up. She had hit her head on the brick wall, and that was the thud I'd heard. After determining she was going to be okay, I began to giggle. All I could think of was her "Oh! (*thud*)" and I would start laughing harder.

"Oh, for goodness' sake Heather, stop that," she said, but she betrayed herself by starting to giggle too. I sat right down beside her and leaned up against the wall, and we both laughed so hard we cried until she finally felt like she was okay to get up again.

These stories and the time she knocked herself out on the trunk lid of my little sister, Sarena's car always come up when we're together. Sarena and I laugh until we cry, and Mom fusses at us good-naturedly. "I was lying half in and half out of her trunk, knocked smooth out, and all she could do was laugh until she cried. You two should be ashamed of yourselves," she would say before she started laughing with us. Later when I dealt with my Lucille Ball Moments and tried not being mortified with embarrassment over them, it was her examples that helped me see them for what they are: funny.

My mom kept a garden that was probably half an acre. If I'm exaggerating, it isn't by much. She cooked three meals a day for about thirteen grown men on our crew. She would throw a load of dishes in the dishwasher and then wash everything else by hand. When she was done, she would throw in a load of laundry and head to the garden. The only time I remember her watching TV was while she was folding clothes.

One day as she was washing dishes by hand, elbow deep in suds, I remember walking up all out of sorts about something. I knew I probably shouldn't even ask, but I said, "Mom will you just hold me for a minute?" I was maybe about five years old, and even that little, I remember watching her make that decision. I remember seeing all the things she still needed to do cross her mind. I could see it on her face. When she opened her mouth to answer me, I really expected to hear that she couldn't. But she took one hand and began to peel all of the suds down her arms and said, "Yes, let's go do that." She took me to the living room without any TV, just the radio playing in the kitchen. We sat down in the rocking chair, and I was probably asleep within five minutes. But I remember feeling her still-damp arms wrap me up and the comfort it gave me to be held. I knew how much hard work was valued, but there were many moments like this from her and my dad that showed me the family was the priority.

They taught me to have confidence in myself. On an entirely different visit that happened to be billy goat-free, I remember my mom or dad calling me into the living room, perching me on the end table, and telling me to show Wendell how well I could sing "Delta Dawn" by Tanya Tucker. I did it y'all. I belted out that song from beginning to end with all the confidence a country girl of six could muster. The entire thing, and that poor man had to sit there and grin at me the whole time. Of course, he also had to clap when I was done and tell me it was wonderful to increase his opportunity of selling something to my parents! Poor guy. My mom and dad were just grinning from ear to ear. Back then I thought they were just proud of me. Now that I'm older, what was the look in their eyes? That could have been wisdom, knowing I had just reinforced confidence in myself to speak and perform in front of others and knowing it would help me out a lot in my growing years. They were pretty good at instilling things like that in us through sneaky, unconventional ways.

Finally, when I was probably a freshman, Dad actually cussed at me one day when I was driving the riding lawn mower like a NASCAR driver around the yard. "Slow that damn thing down and give it a chance to cut!" I know today damn really isn't even considered a cuss word, but to hear it fly out of my dad's mouth towards me was a big deal.

I was shocked, offended, scared, and embarrassed that I had done something that he needed to cuss at me for. This felt like a major rejection. Two things came out of that moment in my life. First of all, to this day, I cannot drive any mower very fast. Every time I inch that gear shift up there, I hear him yelling at me, and I back it down so that the gear shift is closer to the turtle than it is the rabbit, even though I'm definitely a rabbit. I stay controlled.

The second thing is that that phrase has resonated through my life in everything. I've had to choose to slow our lives down multiple times over the years of raising kids to slow down our obligations and give our lives a chance to "cut": a chance to cut memories into their little hearts instead of just check-marking boxes and completing busy activities. I slow myself down to reach out to my grandmother or a long-distance friend or to build a fort in the woods out behind our house with my youngest daughter and try (unsuccessfully every time) to out-fish my older daughter at bass fishing in some backwoods pond we hike to. I slow down to intentionally drive the hour it takes to just hang out with my other daughter some afternoons so that my three grandkids see me and have memories of me being in their home as a natural thing. I have also carved out time to take my third daughter to Bar Harbor, Maine, because it was a dream of hers. That's the good stuff: slowing down and actually giving life a chance to "cut." I highly recommend it: five out of five stars.

In 1996, I was eight weeks pregnant with my fourth daughter when my dad was "sent home to die." The doctors proclaimed that there was nothing left they could do to battle his illness. His body was done. I wanted so much to come up there and be in the home when he passed, but Mom and Dad said no. I still get goosebumps when I remember his voice telling me this, and it is possible it's the last conversation we had.

"Heather, my spirit is leaving this family. But God has already given his permission for our family to go on with the spirit of that little one you're carrying. God already knows if it is a boy or girl, what its name is, and he has a plan. I don't want you being at my side and getting so upset when I pass on that you could miscarry that little promise." We exchanged a few more thoughts and heartfelt I-love-yous, and that was it. It was the last humanly time I heard my dad speak to me.

I learned that love, laughter, a few pranks, and mountains of time spent together are more valuable than any bank account or vacation. I've told you about that Nuttall laugh. You'd be surprised to know that my dad didn't really have it. He had five brothers, and several of them have the loud Nuttall laugh—my brothers have it for sure—but my dad? He would mostly laugh silently, and his face would turn so red it was almost purple. He would chuckle out loud, but by the time it escalated to a full-blown laugh, it was pretty silent, and he was purple.

Slow it down and give that damn thing a chance to cut. I'm trying dad. I'm trying. And there are not enough words in the English language to match my grieving heart having to do it without you.

CHAPTER 6

BECOMING A RUNNER

—

How many times does something from your past carry into your adulthood, affecting who you are or what you'll do? Every dang time, right? Well, I've never believed myself to be a runner because of a moment in junior high track. A specific moment might have well etched in stone that Heather Nuttall is not a good runner, never will be. Maybe it etched into my heart and brain that I would never be a good runner, but a stone tablet would have seemed totally appropriate to me if it had dropped from the sky as well.

    I originally joined the track team because when you have an athlete's heart and an off-season, it's what you do: You find whatever sport is available to you during that season and you join right up! I love athletics of all kinds. I love watching sports and participating in them. I realize that sports in the eighties were a lot different than they are today, but back then you weren't forced to pick just one sport and be hyper-focused on only that sport. I played everything I could: basketball, volleyball, and track were the sports offered to girls then, and I went from one to the next without much of a break all year long. In between, even though my schedule was already busy, I was also the statistician and manager for the boys' basketball team because I just loved being on the go and attending sporting events.

Running wasn't my favorite. At the time, I felt like maybe I was okay at it because in basketball, I could hold my own and was never the last one down the court. Every time my coach said, "on the line," we all knew we were about to run ladders—known back then as "suicides" —until we either threw up or passed smooth out. I could run those. I never really came in first, but I would be in the top three finishers every time. I was confident in this and never questioned my ability to "run" because I could hold my own on the basketball court. Maybe it was just the drive to keep up and not be outdone, but I could always be found somewhere in the middle of a breakaway, and I hated ever getting beat on defense, so it didn't happen very often. I just kept going. I don't claim to be a great athlete; I just never quit.

When track rolled around my first year in junior high, I joined without ever giving it a second thought. It's what I do. I'm a Nuttall; I participate in sports. Every day, practice started out with a one-mile warm-up run. We left the gym and ran a square circuit ending back up at the school. On the very first day, I discovered this was, in fact, not like running ladders. There was no cute little break while the other side of the gym participants ran their turn. This was a nonstop, no catching your breath, suck it up buttercup kind of movement, and I was pretty sure I was not cut out for it. I was 100 percent sure I didn't like it.

This brought a little guilt because my whole family were great track stars. I felt like I was letting the genetics from the Bush and the Nuttall families down. My dad, two of my uncles (one from each side), and another guy won the mile relay at the South Dakota state track meet in 1955 and set a state record. That state record held for several years, and the school record on that mile relay held for almost twenty. While visiting with one of those relay members recently, he said "Your dad was fast but not quite as fast as his brother. But maybe his brother wasn't that much faster, he was just too damn stubborn to ever let anyone beat him. Ever! We never lost once those Nuttall boys moved to town."

I couldn't find an annual proving it as we were missing two years, but my dad was also a state champion at the 110 m hurdles as well. There was a newspaper clipping calling him "The Agar Antelope." If you've ever seen antelope clear a fence, you could get a visual for my dad and those hurdles, according to my mom. Regardless, it appeared that the magic running gene had skipped a generation in my case.

Typically for the warm-up mile, everyone tried to run together in a big group, and no one was concerned about coming in first. One day while running together on this warm-up mile, one of my best friends shot an arrow right through my heart. Okay fine, right through my pride. This girl was always kind; she was one of two girls who had always tried to come to my birthday parties growing up, one of the girls who always tried to be my friend. She was quiet—compared to me everyone was quiet—but our friendship came easy because she liked my crazy and I liked her calm. I'd seen her be stubborn or want her way, but I hadn't really ever seen her do something on her own that would hurt somebody else on purpose. We ran side by side for about three quarters of the circuit when she said to me:

"Heather, I'm really sorry but your breathing makes me so tired I just can't run beside you. I'll see you back at the gym, okay?" With that being said, she kicked it into high gear and left me and the rest of the pack running together behind. Certainly, anyone even kind of close by had to of had heard what she said and watched her run on ahead. If I could have dropped through a manhole in the road at that very moment, it would have been a blessing.

I was so embarrassed. I kept running with the pack. I had no choice. I was basically trying to hold my breath the rest of the way and was close to passing out by the end. We all made it back to the gym, and the team headed outside. She went with the long-distance runners, and I went with the middle-distance group. I didn't have to pretend I wasn't about to cry. I knew I struggled, but to know I affected other people as well was pretty much humiliating. I mean, okay, so I wheezed like a forty-year smoker running a marathon, but I didn't know it would hurt those around me as well! Knowing that everyone running together had most likely heard what she said, my confidence ran somewhere down to the bottom of my shoe and took up fighting for residence with my little toe, and it was winning. That was an embarrassment I didn't want to ever have to redo.

I finished out the track season because in my family, once you committed to something, you didn't just back out. I ran the 400 yd dash and the mile relay, and I did alright. I never finished dead last, but I never finished first either. During the relay, I decided if my breathing could affect other people well, maybe I should use it to my advantage during a race. I submitted to my body's natural tendencies and wheezed all the way around, trying desperately to never let anyone pass me before I could hand off that baton. There were times tripping someone could have been a legitimate option just to keep that from happening but whatever. Sometimes I was able to pass a competitor, but mostly I just held the line and depended on the anchor to save our little squad with a speedy kick at the end. Once the season ended, I never looked back. Track was not for me.

I've always had it in the back of my mind that I would like to do a 5K, but then I'm transported right back to my wheezing seventh-grade self, and I ended up coming up with one excuse or another not to finish this goal.

When COVID-19 hit, we had a lot of time at home. I had a treadmill in a spare bedroom, and I decided: what the heck, I might as well! I figured it didn't matter if I went slow, it didn't matter if I wheezed; doing something would be better than sitting on the couch scrolling on Facebook. So, I crawled on there, and I started with a half-mile warm-up walk. After my muscles were loosened up, I ran through one song, walked the next song, and kept alternating until I wore completely out. Pretty soon, I got to where I could run two songs and then walk one song.

The treadmill was facing a window without a curtain. Because I ran at night a lot, I could see my reflection in that window. I told myself I would always remember how much of the window my reflection took up, remember how much fat I felt jiggling, and just keep going to see what I could do. After a while, I was able to run/walk six miles at a time! That was when I decided if I could do that, I could tighten it up and run a 5K. So, I began training. I ran/walked outside and on the treadmill. Over time, my reflection in the window was taking up less square footage, and there was significantly less jiggling!

When I shared on social media that I had begun running, the support system I gained was amazing and incredibly helpful. I had friends encouraging me and sharing songs they loved to run to, breathing techniques, favorite socks, and styles of shoes.

I signed up for my first 5K: Rooster Days in Broken Arrow, Oklahoma. Every runner I talked to said not to stress about it. They swore there would be some people who just walked the entire event so just do me and do whatever I could without pressuring myself for unrealistic finish times. I wasn't sure I believed this, but it gave me a glimmer of hope that I would not finish dead last anyway! Always got to look for that silver lining!

On the day of the event, I had not told anyone on social media it was happening. My husband was the only one who came with me. I did not need the pressure of knowing anyone was waiting to hear how it went; it made me much calmer. Corey was very supportive and looked after my every need.

So there we were, socially distanced and lined up to start. When the gun sounded, I tried to get to just the right spot and see how far I could go. Several people stopped and walked before I did and sure enough, everyone who lined up at the back of the pack were strictly walkers. There was one bicycle in the first group, and I had no idea what that was all about, but I was glad he was ahead of me so he wouldn't run me over. I had never seen a pace bicycle before, but it lapped me a few times in our weird circle track. The teenager with boundless energy who was always on his heels finished first in something like eighteen minutes. Whatever mister, move along with your six-minute self, you have a wheezing fifty-year-old trying not to die here.

Just about the time I thought I might need to walk, I knew I was breathing heavily, but I also just wanted to keep going for my pride's sake. As I was passing a lady on my right, you're never going to guess what she said to me. She looked over at me with an annoyed yet slightly concerned look on her face and said:

"Are you alright? Your breathing is a little funny."

What the what? Now it was my turn to shoot her a look of slight annoyance. "Yes?" I huffed at her with narrowed eyebrows. She almost immediately pulled up and started walking. I was happy to be rid of her. Could she have said anything closer to what was in my memory bank from junior high? Immediately all the old self-doubt, self-loathing, and all the other negative "self" emotions jumped on my back like a spider monkey. It wasn't very long before I had to stop and walk.

With one simple question, she had taken me out. My mental headspace was all of a sudden in turmoil. Her comment pulled out all the old self-doubt and insecurities that seem to hide somewhere within me, waiting for the moment to pounce.

This event, the one I had been looking forward to, proud of myself for trying, and the newest challenge I wanted to conquer suddenly became a battleground of negative emotions. The mental challenge was definitely much harder than the physical challenge at that point. I kept looking around for that heifer because dadgummit, I wasn't in junior high anymore and insecurities weren't going to win today! Hadn't anyone told her to keep her thoughts to herself? Didn't she watch Disney's *Bambi* after all? "If you don't have anything nice to say, don't say anything at all!" I walked a little bit longer than I should have, and here she comes. She pulls up on my right again and she's running.

It's moments like these I have to decide if I am brave enough to fight my demons or not. I was. I am. If there's anything I am, it's strong. So, as she pulls up even with me, I started to match her pace. Then I pick it up and left her behind. She represented every thirty-eight-year-old "You can't do this" demon for me. She was never allowed to pull up on my shoulder again for the remainder of the race.

Just like in life, I probably wouldn't have been able to do it alone. You see, there was another runner out there that day. He was a man who looked a lot like Wilt Chamberlain, the professional basketball player from years ago. He had to be in his upper sixties, and for the love of Pete, that man had some long legs! He was probably about six-foot-seven, and I would say approximately six feet of him was legs. We didn't test the theory, but I really felt like he could step right over the top of me without any worry of harm. He had great eye contact and words of encouragement each time we met up, either passing on a turn of the race or just finding each other again because of our walk/run needs. As we passed each other on what felt like a traffic circle, he reached out and high-fived me. He absolutely battled my demons with me that day. I never got his name, but I would have loved to thank him.

Since then, I've run a couple of virtual 5Ks as COVID concerns rose and everything went virtual again, but it's just not the same without some heifer representing all of my insecurities pushing me to overcome. Pshhh ask me if I'm okay because of my breathing . . . ugh!

Of the few supporters I had in this journey for running, one was an old friend from high school. She came to our school system after the "I Hate Heather Nuttall Club," if you're wondering. She encouraged me, sent me clips of running techniques, gave me pointers, and we shared music back and forth that we each enjoyed running to. One day while visiting over the phone, I said, "I miss the beach. We should meet up in Florida somewhere and run together!" The speed with which we planned that trip was truly impressive! By February, two South Dakota teenagers were once again seeing each other for the first time in thirty-two years. This time we were women, but the friendship came easy again. We were up each morning around 7:00, walking and running on the beach or through neighborhoods.

One morning, we walked and talked solving world problems, then we started running, and by the time we made it back to the condo before 10 a.m., we had already logged sixteen thousand steps. I'm still a beginner compared to her half-marathon self, but we did it. That time spent with her was healing and wonderful.

The beach did a number on my feet, and I had blisters everywhere. They were on the bottoms of my feet, toes, heels, sides, you name it. My feet looked like a science experiment gone wrong, but I didn't care! I was with a friend, and our times running/walking on the beach were precious. I was going to keep going! A couple of weeks later, when my middle toenail fell off because of the giant blister I had put under it, I sent her a picture of my feet and said, "Isn't that the hottest thing you've ever seen?"

She replied with "Hey that's awesome, I don't ever want to hear you say again that you're not a runner. Those are runners' feet if I ever saw one!"

And just like that, someone from junior high healed my wounded soul from a comment made by another in junior high almost forty years ago. I may not be a great runner, but I am a runner.

I'm going to keep pushing back barriers, whether they are from my distant, not-so-distant, or the recent past. I'm going to wheeze right by anyone who questions me and just keep going. I don't know what happened to that ol' heifer, but

I hope even she finds a way to break the emotional barriers in her heart that pop up from time to time!

Oh, and for the record, she's probably not a heifer at all, but you know, at that moment, my wounded heart was positive she was exactly that. I think it's probably human nature to assign blame on someone who reminds you of something unpleasant but oooooooweeeeeee, she sure picked the wrong tone of voice to use when telling me I breathed funny that day.

I'm still running to this day. I have a very hard time thinking I'm a good runner, but at least now I can call myself a runner. That's progress for me.

CHAPTER 7

50-SOMETHINGS AND TATTOOS

If you grew up in the Midwest, in the seventies, in church, you were taught that if you had tattoos, you were going to hell. Unless you were a Marine. Somehow my mom had decided it was okay for the old Marines walking around town, but I knew even if I went to the Marine Corps, she would not accept this for me! This is another topic I had to search out for myself.

So, before I got any tattoos that would be visible, I went to my mom out of respect. I was searching God for his answer, but it was also very important to me that I not do anything to cause legitimate grief to the woman who had sacrificed her whole life for the five of us kids. We discussed the people we knew who had them. She mentioned someone who had some. She believed their tattoos were very beautiful pieces of art in and of themselves, but she still didn't believe in getting them. I asked her point-blank. "If I get a tattoo that you can see, will it hurt our relationship, will it be something that just grieves your heart every time we see each other?" I also told her that if her answer was yes, I'd probably still get them, but would make sure they would be easily and naturally covered by clothing until she had gone on to heaven and at that point, it would be a free-for-all. She laughed and said that was exactly what she would've expected from me on this topic and that it didn't surprise her a bit. She ultimately said that she respected and appreciated me coming to her first, but no she wouldn't love me any less because of it and it wouldn't hurt our relationship. She just needed to be able to have the chance to speak that she didn't support them.

The main verse used in church settings against tattoos is that pesky verse in Leviticus 19:28.

Ye shall not make any cuttings in your flesh for the dead, nor print any marks upon you: I am the LORD.

Leviticus 19:28 KJV (Holy Bible App)

So the first thing that called out to me here is that I was not in any way, shape, or form trying to call up the dead. All the commentaries I studied referred to the phrase "for the dead" as part of a ritual of black magic trying to call the dead back to the living. Listen to me clearly, I love my dad with all my heart, but if somehow he got "called up" and appeared before me, I would first panic and probably punch him right in the nose out of straight-up fear, and then I'd run and run and run. I just ain't into that black magic, *Pet Semetery* (Stephen King) kind of thing. The movie *Pet Semetery* pretty much cured me of ever wishing beloved humans or animals could have a chance of being brought back to life (*shudder*).

The second thing I noticed about people spouting this is that they could only quote that "God said don't get tattoos." To me, this usually signals that they haven't discussed it with God themselves. They are typically just repeating whatever people they love have told them.

We've established that in this verse, God is addressing the culture at the time to cut yourself repeatedly until you bled and make marks on your body as a sign of mourning or desire to call up the dead. No one teaching or quoting that scripture brings up the part about calling up the dead. That's a funny thing because I also noticed if it were a male telling me these things, none of them wore sideburns. They all shaved them off their face. The verse right before the tattoo one says:

"You shall not shave around the sides of your head, nor shall you disfigure the edges of your beard." Leviticus 19:27 NKJV (Holy Bible iPhone App)

I got to researching and reading that book. It also says that we can't wear clothing of blended material. So I think it's clear that the book of Leviticus addresses issues of the culture at that time and somewhere along the way we have decided it doesn't apply to us. It was also given to us to point out the sheer inability for mankind to be able to "work" their way to salvation. It's a guide to show that no one can be perfect. I went to the authority and prayed about it.

I read and prayed for months and didn't get any word from God saying I couldn't proceed. The first tattoo I got was on my side so that no one would see it. I needed to test this out to see if I felt comfortable in my own skin with art permanently on it. The tattoo is five stalks of wheat symbolizing my girls. There are sprigs of lavender in the bouquet, and it's tied with a purple ribbon, with no significance except that I thought it was pretty. Beside it in my cursive handwriting, it says "Girlsx5." I loved it, and I regretted a little bit that I couldn't show people. You can't just randomly walk up to someone and pull your shirt up without the person on the receiving end feeling a little uncomfortable after all. I had this one for about a year and a half before I decided that I wanted one that showed. I chose my wrist.

This story brings up probably one of the biggest, almost permanent Lucille Ball Moments in my entire life. Thank goodness it did not end up being permanent because wow!

I love flowers. My dad always gave the women in his life roses. My mom never lacked for big, beautiful bouquets, and we girls always got at least one red rose from him every Valentine's Day or on birthdays. Also, beside my dad's headstone is a giant peony bush that my mom planted. She loves it and will someday rest beside it. These two things have created a love for these specific flowers in my heart. So, I chose a rose and peony wrist tattoo with my life verse written in my handwriting underneath.

I communicated with the tattoo artist, we emailed and drew up designs together, and I gave him the verse Mark 14:10.

My life verse is simply this: "She did what she could...." (Jesus speaking) Mark 14 NIV (Holy Bible App)

The day I found this verse, it was like Jesus was saying it about me, straight to me. Right then, I adopted it as my life verse. Always being hypersensitive to rejection, I've repeatedly beat myself up for not being good enough. I just have to rest in the fact that given all the circumstances, I did what I could, every time.

This verse was a giant reliever of guilt and unattainable expectations for me. I never really feel like I do a great job at any event. I'm good at many things, but not super great at any one thing. I'm a little impulsive, a little scatterbrained, a little this and a little that. If you ever got a glimpse inside my brain, you'd be so impressed that I can function daily! There are always several dozen thoughts rolling around in my head like squirrels packing for winter, and at any moment, I can chase one of those thoughts down a rabbit hole as if I'm entering Alice's Wonderland. Once I enter Wonderland . . . well, it's a long stay.

When it comes to life and the people I love, I have always loved big and loved hard. I give everything I am to help others succeed. When my girls were chasing competitive softball, I worked outside the home and I sold whatever I thought I could sell just so we could afford the $300 bats, the latest catcher's gear, the coolest cleats; the list goes on and on. I wanted my girls to feel the part as well as playing the part. I made all the practices, games, and tournaments, and none of the sacrifices could ever compare to watching them hit a home run, three-run double, or catching every pitch of a nineteen-inning game.

We chased them until we lost ourselves. We were always over committed, overwhelmed, over budget, and just over in general. I always felt five minutes late, five dollars short, and I never felt like I was enough for the ones I loved. I never felt like any party I threw was planned well enough; I could've done better. I could've done more. I could've . . . Remember from the seventies, "Coulda, shoulda, woulda?" That was my life on repeat, and it was a heavy load.

So back to the very public tattoo parlor. We had the flowers; we had the verse. He printed it out, sprayed my arm, and laid it all out right where we wanted. But at the last second, he hesitated, and he said, "We should always double-check things like verses before we commit them forever, right?" Um, yes, that sounds reasonable, right? Y'all . . .

Mark 14:10 is in fact:

"And Judas Iscariot, one of the twelve, went unto the chief priests, to betray him unto them." **Mark 14:10** KJV (Holy Bible App 10)

No, no, no, no! Obviously, I gasped without concern for how many people were nearby. I had a tiny nervous breakdown over the fact I almost carried Judas Iscariot on my arm forever. I mean it's not like you could easily turn a ten into an eight without having to mess up the entire tattoo. At this point, the entire tattoo parlor is giggling at my ridiculousness, my husband is trying to find a chair to crawl under, and my soul is literally wrinkled. Have you ever had your soul wrinkle? I imagine it would feel a little like watching your own hand get run over by a car, but only this happens in your head. It happens, it hurts, and it's incredibly embarrassing!

Mark 14:8, 14:8, 14:8! I will never again forget (even without looking at my correct tattoo) Mark 14: EIGHT.

"She did what she could. ......" **Mark 14:8** NIV (Holy Bible App)

The story is that a woman was in possession of a costly flask of oil. It's not explained why or how she had gotten it, but when she saw that it was Jesus, she broke the flask and poured it on his head. This was an honored ritual performed back then, anointing someone with oil. Some were very upset because in their opinion, she wasted the oil, and it should have been sold for the money it was worth and the money given to the poor. "These offended people criticized her sharply," verse 5 says. In verse 6, Jesus defends her, "Let her alone. Why do you trouble her? She has done a good work for Me."

Verse 8 goes on with Jesus defending her, saying "She has done what she could. She has come beforehand to anoint My body for burial." Verse 9 goes on to say that "Wherever this gospel is preached in the whole world, what this woman has done will also be told as a memorial to her." An eternal memorial? Just for doing what she could. A release fell on me, and I realized that even though sometimes others disagreed with me, or I didn't have everything I needed for the moment to be grandiose, I always did what I could. Jesus loved her for that. I began to be able to love myself a little more knowing that's how Jesus felt about women who simply did what they could every time.

So even though I'm the scatterbrained lady who almost carried Judas Iscariot around on her wrist forever, I was settling in on being okay with being the woman who did what she could every time. The whole point is, I challenged something I'd been taught my whole life. Was getting a tattoo something God would shout against immediately and loudly? No. For me, it turned out to be something that led me to my life verse and a release from living under the expectations and pressures from others.

Ultimately, I got my answer from God instead of just swallowing the things people had assumed from scripture or passed down from generation to generation. I challenged things I'd always thought. Sometimes when I do this, I find these things are in fact, facts. Other times, I've found that while God lays it on someone's heart to abstain from activities, he may not give the same directive to others. In short, some things aren't forbidden for everyone; just the few he has set apart for something else. It's up to each one of us to find out directly from him where our freedoms lie, not necessarily from man-made interpretations that get passed down for many generations.

To mark my fiftieth birthday, I got my third tattoo: the latitude and longitude of my childhood farm tattooed across my shoulder with a wheat head at the top because farm life and all I learned there are just pretty precious to me. Of course, this one is easily covered and only makes public appearances in warm weather. But I finally have a visible symbol of the farm life that made me who I am. The latitude and longitude of my childhood farm is just simply for all of the warm fuzzies it brings me when I see it.

My husband has remarked many times when seeing it that he is jealous. He doesn't have any specific location with a latitude and longitude that means anything to him. Nothing as important as the farm is to me that he could use as a tattoo of his own. He says he hopes I realize how special it is that I have one. I do. Memories of that farm make me smile every time.

CHAPTER 8

THE DAY THE MUSIC DIED

There've been many days when the music died in my life. It could be the New Year's Eve we let our two older girls invite roughly 3,700 kids over for a party. My husband was in the throes of addiction, and by the time forty or so middle to high school kids had shown up, my partner, my bouncer, my "Mister Fun Guy" was incapacitated; and that's downplaying it so dramatically I feel all unwound not giving you the whole picture. That's for another book and another time, though.

So, me . . . just me. I'm running around our property, confiscating marijuana from kids, pulling other kids out from under a truck trying to get after the horizontal hokey pokey (I mean there are just so many things wrong with that location for sex!) I felt like I needed to talk to this child about her critical thinking and decision-making skills, but I didn't have time! I also felt like a good talk with my girls might be in order. If these were the decisions their friends were making on the topic of sex, a good once-over on the subject may be beneficial. Good grief!

Some of the kids had locked a boy in the monkey cage. Don't ask, but we really did have a monkey cage: no monkey, but yes, monkey cage. We had allowed them to cast a wide net when inviting people, and this proved to be a very regrettable decision. While discussing this event with my daughter recently, she said she had literally just walked up and down the halls of the school shouting "Party at my house!" and giving up the address. That certainly explains the number of kids and the activities that happened there that evening.

I was in the kitchen, trying to be a ridiculous version of the perfect "Pinterest Mom," a real June Cleaver, if you will, baking dozens of chocolate chip and peanut butter cookies, crying because I was overwhelmed by all of these kids and watching over them by myself. I was feeling very alone. Here I was again, trying to pull off what should have been a normal event for my children, but everything was out of control, and it was just magnifying all of my feelings of inadequacies. My husband was in the worst shape I had ever seen him in. Previously, even through bad times, we were always a team; we could put everything aside to work together for whatever needed to be done. Tonight, I was on the court alone and very outmatched.

Someone asked me why I didn't just stop the party. I sat there with my mouth wide open and finally had to say, "This sounds incredibly stupid, but it never even crossed my mind. I was so busy juggling one thing after another, I never thought to do that." I was literally surviving from one second to the next. I naively felt that the tongue-lashing I gave out every time I confiscated any contraband had fixed them right up and they wouldn't try that again! Good grief, I was in la-la land trying to hold on that night.

The day before New Year's Eve, I had expected my husband to be in charge of all the flashlight duty needs. Everything that included wandering around outside and monitoring all the shenanigans would be his job. I would be in the kitchen baking cookies, serving punch, monitoring the content being shown on TV, watching over my two youngest girls, and playing bouncer not allowing anyone to wander upstairs. Removing my husband from that scenario because he was messed up just really left me in a situation I couldn't face alone mentally or physically.

I was not totally sure where my two little ones were because there were so many kids I didn't know, and the house was full. I felt like I had "laid down the law" to all the attendees and for all of the regulars that were at my house all the time. I had no worries that the "regulars" would break my "laws" for that evening. We kind of had a routine for how things went at our house established already, and for the most part they honored what we wanted. As the night went on, however, I began to see many kids that I didn't know very well. I was a little bit worried about my younger girls who were probably eight and ten in this large crowd of attendees, so I took some neighborhood kids aside with my girls and instructed them to look out for my "little" ones and to alert me if anyone showed up that should not be trusted.

Several trips through the living room revealed my little ones separated and surrounded by the neighborhood kids and trusted friends. I was so grateful for them and my older girls stepping up to the plate on that one that I was able to go back to Suzy Homemaker and Martha Stewart impersonations to keep up the facade that everything at the Westovers' was hunky-dory.

Corey and I had battled it out heavily before any of the kids had started showing up. I told him that I didn't care what he did, but he was not going to embarrass his kids by hanging around this party, considering the shape he was in. I emphatically told him I didn't care where he went but he just couldn't stay here.

We had a full apartment with a cinder-block basement under it that housed all of his woodworking tools. He had a radio and a chair down there, and he typically liked to hang out there on occasion, so I really thought he would be there. We also had a screen-printing shop on the property where we had a small business on the side. I was assuming he would go to either of these locations and sulk or have another round of his favorite poison. As mad as I was at him, the words we exchanged before the kids started showing up were bad, and they contributed to my tears that evening. I was dying to try and figure out where my husband could have gone off to so he could pass out or possibly hurt himself. Every moment, every emotion was hyper-focused and yet all over the place. Deep breath.

Did I mention I had decided just five days before to leave my husband? I wanted to be that long-suffering wife, the one who picked him up and carried him through his addiction, giving him a reason to live, but it wasn't working, and I was done: D-O-N-E, done.

Did I mention two days after I had decided to leave my husband, I found out I was pregnant with our fifth baby? I hadn't shared it with him or anyone else. I was just in the middle of the biggest crisis of my life and finding out God had chosen me to carry a baby again moved absolutely all of the stable ground beneath my feet.

At that point, it was just me and God. I was afraid that by the time she was born, it really would just be God and me as her parents because my man was just too much of a wildcard. I wasn't sure what was going to happen with Corey. This addiction had a chokehold on him, and I was losing faith in him to win. That was an odd place to be for me. Not having faith in him was like being in a foreign country. He was a wrestler in high school, and I never once had the belief he would lose any match ever. It happened sometimes, but it was always a surprise to me. I was not accustomed to the feeling of not having faith in him but by this night, all of my faith was almost dead.

Having a baby to me was the highest honor that God and a man could bestow on a woman. I would have had a hundred babies if he would have wanted to. When hearing of other husbands begging their wives to have another baby, I always thought it was such an honor. To have your man want a child with you, to ask you to bear his child. I never got that. He never really asked me to marry him, nor did he ever ask to have a child. It wasn't that he didn't want them. I just don't think he ever really thought about it.

The summer after high school, we were discussing life after SBHS (Go Chargers!), and he said we could just live together. I replied with a heartbroken smile. "Oh, then I'm not your girl. That's not how I see my life going." I then told him I didn't see us continuing to date if we knew it was going to end when I headed off to college several states away in August. At that point, he said, "Well I guess we could do the other?" I made him explain. "Marriage. I guess we could get married? I don't want to lose you." Bam: now we were getting married.

We were two very young kids. I had a late summer birthday, and I wasn't even eighteen at this point yet. We were two young kids in a ditch not really knowing what we were doing. He didn't know how to ask, and I wasn't sure how we were going to go forward. All we knew was that we didn't want to lose each other.

It was the same with having children. Once the first one happened, we just continued to let it happen. I knew from growing up in a big family and an even bigger extended family that I wanted that full supper table filled with laughter, love, arguments, and pranks. The last two children were surprises—one more than the other—but neither was unwanted in any way.

The only thing he knew was he absolutely was not going to be the one to get a vasectomy. If I wouldn't get a sterilization procedure and that meant we ended up with seventeen kids, well then. That's what it meant. But I don't ever remember him asking me to have a baby or even necessarily "wanting" another one. He just loved them when they showed up.

So there I was, with other people's daughters trying to lose their virginity under the neighbor's lifted 4x4 truck, confiscating a large supply of marijuana from thirteen- and fifteen-year-olds, baking cookies, rescuing kids from the monkey cage, wondering if tonight would be the night my husband's addiction would finally hurt him irreparably or even cause death, pregnant with my fifth child and the daughter that would be closest in age to her was already nine. We had made it almost a decade, but here we were again: my fourth and fifth children, products of birth control not strong enough for the perfect storm that was my relationship with my husband.

I didn't even wear makeup that night. I can still feel the shirt I wore. It was a long-sleeved pink shirt from the Gap that had long since lost its ability to really look like anything other than a sloppy T-shirt. I had located my two "little ones" and gotten them settled in their room watching something that was what I felt was age appropriate. Freddy Krueger is what the big kids had chosen, and I really didn't want them exposed to horror movies just yet. I left them with a giant stash of popcorn and snacks to last the evening. I later found the remains of the popcorn and snacks all over the staircase where they hid peeking through the banister watching Freddy Krueger anyway. I was too caught up in my real-life nightmare to do a great job of monitoring what they watched that evening. They got away with that one, and I never mentioned it. It was the tiniest of the battles there that evening, and I was at least trying to pick my battles.

Finally, most of the kids still there had settled in the living or dining room where they could see our big screen TV, and they had put their hormones aside. No one was making out or doing any other sexual exploration. I guess I'd finally run off all the kids with marijuana because no one tried to light up in the house, and it appeared that the monkey cage was empty so there was a lull in the chaos.

I went to look for my husband. The details are another story for another time. But as I carried him up the stairs with very little help from him and poured him into our bed, my heart was aching in ways I had never known was possible. He was so under the influence, and I guess the bed was spinning so hard that when I got him into bed flat on his back, he couldn't even stay there. One minute he looked like he was relaxing and then the next second, he was lying on the floor again.

I stood at the foot of our bed watching him in the worst form I'd ever seen him in, knowing I was pregnant and wishing with all my heart I could leave him. At that moment, all of the 3,700 kids downstairs started counting down the New Year. Ten! Nine! Eight! I got dizzy and nauseous, dropped to my knees, and sobbed a little for everything in my soul that was dying and for the man I used to love but who had for all intents and purposes, disappeared . . . and the music in my soul died.

The music dying could have been a few years before when my dad—my confidence in life, the one who just "got me"—was diagnosed with Acute Lymphocytic Leukemia, when he fought for fifteen months and ended up with brain tumors because apparently, diseases like that can retreat from the body where the chemo is attacking it and find refuge in the brain where the effects of chemo are dramatically lessened.

Maybe it was when they "sent him home to die." If I don't ever have to hear that phrase again for the rest of my life, it would be really great. Probably it was October 4, 1996, at about 6:30 p.m. when they called to say he had breathed his last. Again, the music died.

It could have been every day of a decade-long struggle when my spouse was caught up in addiction, when the things he said to me that straight up split my soul. These are things he will never remember because of the amnesia caused by Ambien, but I'll never forget because they hurt so much. Or maybe it was the times when under the influence, he threw me across the room or left bruises on me but never remembered a second of it. In fact, he accused me of making it up and bruising myself to get attention. Maybe on that day, my soul was rent in two, and the music died.

It could have been when one of my children was verbally or sexually harassed or assaulted. Maybe when one of them ran away or when they called me in January at midnight from behind a dumpster, hiding from the guy in their life after things got out of hand. Her fear was so big, I could hear it in her shaky whispering voice, and I was hours away from her. When she said, "Mama, don't say anything. I can hear his footsteps, shh." Every second felt like years. This moment was worse for me than the NYE party or the night my dad died. I was powerless, and my baby was being stalked. The potential for harm was immeasurable, and I was absolutely unable to help her terror. If I could've wiggled my nose and immediately switched places with her, I would have done it in a second. Being on the phone in that moment was more physically and emotionally painful than anything I'd ever been through before. My chest hurt, my arms went weak, and I sat in that chair with every muscle in my entire body flexed as tight as I could waiting out those moments until she was safe again.

When bad things happened to any of my kids and I wasn't enough to save them, heal their hurts, or block all things terrible for the sake of their mental health, it killed me. When I couldn't be everything for my kids my soul wrinkled, and the music died.

Maybe it was when I turned fifty, so looking forward to every day of life, and then I lost two uncles—two of my dad's brothers. They died within a week of each other. Ten months later, my grandmother, Dad's mom died. It was like I was losing him all over again three times within a year. Three more anchors to my soul here on earth were gone so quickly. I realized then that I had far more anchors in heaven than I did on earth, and I was feeling very unprotected here. It was too much, and again the music died.

How did I get to fifty and become the woman I am? Because my life, the whole thing is beautiful. These are but a fraction of the traumas I have experienced or have had to watch loved ones experience. But each moment is a piece, a fraction. When the whole tapestry is woven with the good, the funny, the sorrow, and the tragedy, it's the most beautiful piece that I could have ever been a part of. How am I such a strong woman? I walked through all those things and more, and I made it.

I can tell you the maestro starts the music again. Hope buds inside your soul, and it's as if the first notes on the strings of a cello begin to create the beat the other instruments will join. I've been through a lot, and it's very reassuring to be able to say that if you're still and allow hope to grow again, the music begins to penetrate your soul like a fresh spring wind. Everything will feel alright again.

Oh, I made mistakes along the way for sure. There's a high school here in Oklahoma that for many years had the legend of "Crazy Mama Westover" floating around in it. Some of those moments I'm proud of, some of them I'm not. But one thing I know: I did what I could. When I learned better, I did better. But I always did what I could.

If each of my kids could have agreed to make the same mistake as the others, I'd be a champion mama by now, protecting my kids like a fierce lioness and never making mistakes. Hear me roar! But like the beauty of my story, they are all different. They have all suffered and rejoiced many different things because their tapestries will be unique.

I spent many years believing if I would have been better or more, or maybe if I were skinnier, prettier, funnier, more Pinterest-y, more organized, or just all around super cool, maybe my husband wouldn't have ever taken that first pill. Maybe my daughters wouldn't have had rebellion beating in their veins. Maybe all the times they made bad choices and blamed it on me, maybe they were right. Maybe I just wasn't good enough? It has taken me thirty-one years of adulthood to embrace the truth that I am simply who I am right now. Tomorrow I'll learn more, and I'll be different. But nothing I could've done would've changed the experiences my husband and my kids had to walk through. They had to complete their stories. I am part of theirs, and they are part of mine. We'll get there when we get there, and eventually my story will be over.

I have to let you know though, that husband of mine? I didn't walk out on him. A decade of crisis and I have no idea why I stayed, except I kept praying to God to let me out of my vow I made to him about that man, but God always reassured me that he was taking care of me. As of September 25, 2022, I will have celebrated thirty-four years of anniversaries with him. He beat the pills; he beat the mental battle. Just when I was losing faith in him, thinking the chokehold addiction had on him would win, he beat it. He put all of the hard work in. As I watched him fight, my respect for him soared. I no longer looked at him and felt disgust. Looking at him, all I saw was strength, and I once again felt all the love and pride in the warrior I thought he was back in high school. Overcoming addiction isn't for the weak. The man who has been my best friend for most of the years since I was thirteen years old has been restored. He is still my best friend.

The daughters that did their best to drown themselves in rebellion? Today they are the most beautiful, productive, and wonderful creatures you'll ever meet. I still don't know why God honored me with getting to be their mama.

I just have to be sure that Jesus would look at others and say "She did what she could" when my flaws are proclaimed. When I know better, I'll do better.

CHAPTER 9

THE SNAKE WRANGLER

Is anyone else scared of snakes? I mean, unreasonably scared of snakes? Not only was I traumatized by them over and over as a child, but I'm also pretty sure my fear of snakes traumatized my parents as well.

My family were farmers, but we were also custom harvesters. We got everything we could out of our land, but at about the middle to end of April each year, my dad and all of the hired hands—which included my brothers—would load up all of the equipment and head for Texas and New Mexico. When school let out in May, Mom would bring us girls and join them on the road. They would contract with farmers down there who needed someone to harvest their wheat crops for them. It was a hard, dirty life that consisted of very long days and super short nights. They would harvest as much as they could until it was about time for our crops to be ready in South Dakota, and then we would load up and bring everything back to start working on our fields. It was an amazing way to grow up as a child. Mostly because I could just play and have fun instead of working hard, but nevertheless, I was in the field most of the day right beside everyone else.

One year, when I was probably about five or six years old, I was playing in a West Texas field. The combines had already cut the area I was playing in, so the wheat stalks were just about thigh-high on me. Texas has a species of snake called the Blue Racer. Some say they are curious and love to play in the shade. I believe they stalk you and wait to eat you, but to each their own. As I was playing, I thought I saw a really big wheat stalk just standing straight up, and I remember feeling a warning in my spirit, but also, I was too flighty to recognize I needed to give attention to that feeling. I kept playing, and at one point I had knelt down to dig in the dirt for something. When I stood up, I twisted just a little bit, and there in my shadow was a snake. How big was it you ask? Well, I was just knee-high to a grasshopper so I can unequivocally say to you that this snake was as big as the water tower in town. Period. It's a fact—write it down. Also, realize this is from the perception of a tiny tot, so take that size measurement for what it's worth.

I took off running. He slithered right behind me, keeping up with me and my shadow with ease. I ran left. I ran right. I ran in circles screaming and flailing my arms. Each time I would stop to see if I'd lost him, he would be behind me and he would stand up about two feet and just look back and forth at me. Looking back on it now, I think if it were typical for snakes to wag their tail, he would have been wagging his tail. Every time he rose up in the air and looked at me, it was almost like we were playing some fantastic game he was really, really enjoying. I was doing the opposite of enjoying it. I had tears streaking my dirty little face, and I'm pretty sure there were snot rivers flowing down my chin as well. Come to think of it, I wonder if I was wheezing so much because I had been running after all? I finally made it to one of the pickup trucks and crawled up into the bed of it and looked down. Yep, there he was, raised up to all of his glory and looking at me. I'm sure he was wondering why I wanted to stop playing, but I was busy losing my ever-lovin' mind and establishing a life-long phobia. I was too busy to play.

I finally sobbed and screamed and did a perfect cannonball into the funny farm mental state where I would camp most of my life. Someone eventually heard me and came to rescue me from the little demon. After that I hated snakes; I didn't like them in books, movies, or TV shows. This started a long battle of being able to control my mental thoughts, feelings, and emotions whenever I was exposed to one. Every time I saw one in person and most of the times I saw one on TV, I would have nightmares, sometimes for days.

My mom told me that one day when they took us all out to a pond fishing, I perched myself on a rock and was casting and reeling repeatedly having the time of my life. Then came the moment mom and dad noticed two snakes romping in the grass directly behind me. They didn't know if they were playing or fighting, but it didn't matter. Immediately they both feared what would happen if I saw them. Dad checked it out and made sure they weren't poisonous and then they made the call to just not alert me to the fact two demon nightmares were within arm's reach of me. You see, they wanted to be able to sleep for the next few nights without having to sit up with me, so they left me in the dark! I guess we got through the whole event without me ever noticing! They were so relieved, and everyone slept well that week.

After she told me what had happened, it confirmed to me that God loved me, and we had an unspoken agreement. God would never let me see a snake, even if it was right next to me unless I absolutely needed to see it. I'm not going to lie, I made myself believe that and even counted on it to get myself through. In my head, I might very well have walked right over the top of one hundred snakes through my life, but God blinded me to them because he loved me! Hush, you've told yourself some doozies too, so don't judge me!

The next event I remember makes me giggle... now. Back then, I was busy having a mental breakdown, and it was not funny. At this point, I've been a mom so long that I have loads of sympathy for my mom, and when I think of what she must have been thinking and going through on that night, it makes me laugh right out loud with sympathy for her.

I had just been out to the movies with a group of friends, and we went to see *Indiana Jones and the Raiders of the Lost Ark*. In this movie, there's a feast, and one of the delicacies was a giant snake that had been cooked while being wrapped around a pole. The server comes by and slices it open, and tons of baby snakes fall out, ready to be eaten... (*shudder in revulsion here*). Later, while Indy and crew are trying to make their way through a pyramid or some creepy building, they get stuck in a room full of snakes, and I mean full. These snakes were all sizes, but most of them were tiny. They were skinny and short. I was uncomfortable in the movie theatre, but I was with my friends, and I just remember sitting there white-faced and horrified at the fact this could actually happen to someone (because movies are real y'all, right?). But I recovered quickly, and the rest of the night went off without a hitch. Until about 2 a.m.

In high school, I had the best bedroom ever. I was the only one in the basement. I had a waterbed without baffles and the heating element was the best feature to the whole bed. I drifted on water like I was floating on the river and was lulled to sleep every night—except for this night. I remember waking up pouring sweat. I had just been dreaming about being in that room with Indiana Jones and was convinced I was still there. I did recognize that it was my room, but the dream had been so real that I was still convinced snakes were everywhere. Under my bed I had six storage drawers and there was no convincing me that those drawers weren't full of snakes. I stood up on the waterbed and made my way to the wood frame on the outside. Once I got good footing, I jumped as far as I could to reach my bedroom door, clearing the snake-filled drawers of course. I sprinted upstairs and sat in the living room crying. Mom heard me and came to sit with me. I remember I was sitting on a footstool and rocking back and forth as I sobbed. As I began to tell her about the movie I said, "Mom I'm not kidding, some of them were so little they could easily hide in our shag carpet!" Again, if this were a movie, that was the moment the music would have crashed and spiked in intensity. After saying it out loud, I looked down at that carpet and back at my mom. Then I reached down and started raking through the carpet with my fingers to be sure. My mom then eloquently shouted at me, "Heather Marie, are you on drugs?"

I didn't miss a beat and yelled right back in her face, "No, but I wish I was!" The look on her face betrayed her feelings of disgust and worry, maybe even fear for me at the time.

Back then counseling wasn't really a thing—only if you were really bad. I still don't know why I didn't end up in therapy.

Fast forward to when I got married. We moved to Cheyenne, Wyoming, as two eighteen-year-old newlywed kids. We rented a basement apartment that only had one door going in and out. While trying to unpack and organize the apartment, I tried to push something into the top shelf of the coat closet (right by the front door), and something hissed at me! I screamed and ran back to the kitchen and crawled up on the counter and sobbed and yelled for my man! Here he came with all of his eighteen-year-old splendor, ready to slay dragons for me.

He reached up into the closet, and it hissed again! He got out the shotgun, fully prepared to blow a giant hole in the landlord's wall. Loaded and ready to shoot, he poked the closet a couple more times, each time resulting in angry hissing.

Let me just jump to the end and tell you that he didn't blow a hole in the wall. You should also know that an aerosol can has the ability to sound just like a snake when pressed in a closet. Good grief.

Years later, my cat brought a tiny grass snake into the house, and by the time the evening was over, I was in the hospital giving birth to our second daughter. Fear is a real thing y'all.

I got better about not having nightmares, but I still felt the same way about snakes. One morning when I was about fort-eight, as I was coming out of deep sleep, I heard a voice say to me "You know. You fear snakes more than you trust me?" That's it; it was God. There'd been a couple times in my life that he had spoken to me like that as I was coming awake, and I recognized the message as one that I knew would someday be an issue. Right away, I emailed the Tulsa Zoo and told them about my fear and how it was time; I needed to touch a snake, I needed to be close to one on purpose, and if I were really strong, I needed to hold one. I thought maybe it would rid me of the fear. I canceled that appointment about four times and just stopped answering their emails.

That year, I was a preschool teacher, and one of my kids brought the weekend buddy back with pictures of them together holding his pet snake Lupin. He then asked me if he could bring Lupin for show-and-tell. Now, first of all, this little thing held my heart. He had the most beautiful blue eyes, deepest adorable dimples, and a giggle that lit up the room. I just wanted to squeeze him, he was so cute inside and out. I looked down into his little eyes and panicked about how I could possibly say no to him. Then I got an idea; I told him I would have to ask the director of the preschool. In my head I really felt like no responsible adult in leadership would allow a snake into a building with all of these precious babies. She was my ace in the hole!

I entered her office with all the confidence in the world. She was going to say no. I told her my predicament, and would you believe that woman had the nerve to look up at me smiling and say "Sure, why not? All God's creatures big and small, right Heather?"

Has she lost her mind? Do I need to teach her about Adam and Eve and the serpent? Did her mama skip reading that bible story to her? Good grief. Now I couldn't say no. So much for my ace in the hole! Lupin was scheduled for the following week.

Leading up to that day, I was out at the summer camp I worked for trying to paint some larger rocks so the kids would have fun messages to find as they walked the grounds. It was fall, and the leaves had been falling. I knew the dangers. I swished the leaves back and forth a little bit looking for snakes, and I sat down straddling a rock that I had decided to paint. A little bit into my creativity, I felt something bump my foot. I looked down and I was stepping on a snake! Again, my soul wrinkled. It hurts y'all. It was birthing season for timber rattlers in our part of the country, and I had found myself one. Luckily, I had stepped on so much of him that he wasn't able to strike above my tennis shoe to get to my skin, but he was angry and giving it his best shot . . repeatedly.

I called my boss up at the office who I trusted to rescue me from my demon, and told him my predicament. He came and saved me, and that baby snake would never grow up to frighten anyone else. I knew my deal with God had come to an end, and now I was seeing all the snakes all the time. I had to deal with this. Next week couldn't come soon enough!

Then came the day Lupin entered my classroom. I was afraid, with internal shivers, and I was a wreck thinking I was going to have to model courage in front of all these babies who loved and looked up to me. My student and his dad taught the class all about snakes and how to feed them. Then came the moment the dad looked up at me and said, "Are you ready to hold him?"

Y'all . . . no! I was never actually going to be ready! But I shook my head yes and held my hands out to hold my main nemesis. I freaked out and ran away a little the first time he tried to hand him to me. Another little student leaped from his chair and raced to me, wrapping his arms around my thigh and giving me a fierce hug. "You can do it, Mrs. Westover!" Back to it I went. I had already imagined that when the dad handed this thing to me, it would take one look at me, strike, and bite me squarely between the eyes, but I had to tell fear to hush for the sake of these kiddos. He placed Lupin in my hands. Lupin could've cared less about me; he twisted around and reached up toward my student as if seeing that little boy brought him comfort. Immediately my student turned both his amazing eyes and his dimples in my direction and said, "Wook at him Mrs. Westover!" with all the love a child feels for their pet.

I "wooked" at him and immediately handed him back to Dad. But I did it! I didn't have nightmares that night!

Sometimes conquering fear is just simply standing up to it once. Other times, it takes a little perseverance. In cases like mine, it takes forty-nine years to finally work its way out. To be honest, I would have never been open to facing that phobia ever had God not spoken to me and then presented opportunities to let me know it was time.

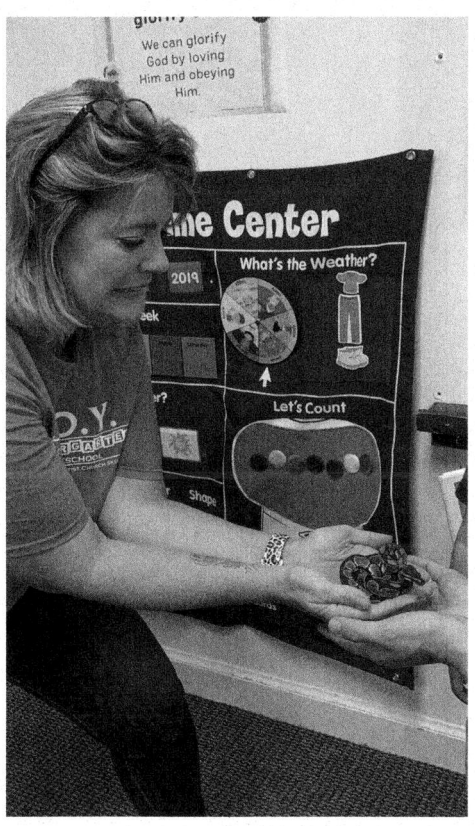

I'm not totally free from fear of snakes today, but I'm not controlled by the fear anymore either. I still get the hot flash adrenaline rush, immediate sweats, shaky limbs, and rush of panic. But I'm able to control it now, and it doesn't control me. Each exposure is an intentional walking out of facing the fear that wants to come "home" each time it happens, but I'm now able to consistently answer the door and shoo it away like you would any pest hanging around your yard.

CHAPTER 10

THE OBSTACLE COURSE CALLED HIGH SCHOOL

Rejection, fear of snakes, self-loathing, insecurities, and fake confidence for days: sounds like a recipe for success, right? High school was an obstacle course for me. Still reeling from the "I Hate Heather Nuttall Club," I wasn't sure who really liked me for me and who didn't even a few years later entering high school. I felt like I was walking on thin ice all the time. There was a cute new boy by the name of Corey Westover my freshman year. He was a great distraction from many of my insecurities. He played football and participated in wrestling. He was patient, cute, and always made time for me.

Partying became a thing, and I kind of struggled here. Drinking was not accepted in the Nuttall house, not at all—except for the big bottle of Jim Beam in the cabinet beside the dishwasher for when you had a cold and needed a Hot Toddy. Other than that, it was a no-go. There isn't one single beer made then or now that I like. I felt the need to fit in, and everybody drank at these parties, but I couldn't do it. Just the taste of beer sent me to dry heaving beside my car one night.

This is actually another taboo life topic if you grew up in church in the Midwest in the seventies and eighties. Alcohol made you lose control of your senses, and you would not be in control of yourself and then you'd end up acting a fool everywhere you went, right? That's what we were told! But like all teenagers, we had the "It won't happen to me" disease, and each one of us had to try it out for ourselves. I swear on the first day of high school, half of my classmates had already thrown their guts up from a night of Fireball Festivities. Except it was more like an Everclear Event because . . . you know . . . we were all broke. I was always jealous of the Catholic kids because it appeared to this teenager anyway that drinking was accepted. My Baptist-self had a harder time navigating this situation. Pretty much, I had to choose to be the good church girl or embrace sin when it came to alcohol. I really wish I would've known I could go straight to God for things back then. I thought this was a one-and-done parental rule. If your parents said no, it was a sin, the end. Choosing to do it brought heaps of condemnation. God would most certainly have told me no at that age, but my brain just attached it as forever sinful, and I assumed it would never be addressed again.

The first time I ever drank was with the foreign exchange student that my parents had brought in. Like all proper teenage girls, I complained about all the perceived injustices in my life. I have four siblings; the older ones are six to eleven years older than me, and my little sister is eleven years younger than I am. I never had anyone to hang out with and felt incredibly shorted in the companion category. So Mom, doing what moms do, tried to right this wrong. She brought in a foreign exchange student from Holland, and I quickly had another painful lesson in being careful what you ask for.

I was thirteen, and everything about her was different. I'm not sure what I expected when I learned she would be coming from Holland after all. She had the just shrug her shoulders and ignore everything attitude about everything. Part of me was so impressed with that. The other part of me stayed horrified. Everyone knew we were now "family." She decided to go out for basketball because I played. During practices, she always wore a T-shirt, and I had never seen certain parts of her body before one fateful evening.

The night of the first basketball game was the first time I really realized that some foreign countries never shave—ever. She would run down the court, raise both of her arms up in the air, and yell "Me! Me! Pass to me!" I'm not sure why I hadn't noticed before, but right there in that basketball game with our sleeveless jerseys was the first time I ever knew that females could grow armpit hair just as long as the guys'. I had seen her hairy legs, and it was a turnoff, but I had thought, "Meh, just another crazy foreign thing." You could also see all the other Midwest eighties teenage girls on the team trying to wrap their brains around seeing her armpits as well. Not being too far away from the "I Hate Heather Nuttall Club" trauma, I was so worried that everyone would make fun of her and then by proxy, me.

I went home complaining and moaning to my parents, and they were sympathetic and also a little unnerved because they had never seen a girl like this either! After a couple of months, I think my mom went out and bought her every kind of shaver or razer there was on the market, wrapped it up in a gift, took her out for a restaurant dinner together, and presented her this gift with the talk about "I know it's never fun to get made fun of, and I've noticed some of the kids snickering at the basketball games. If you're comfortable trying something new, I bought all these options you can choose from to be able to shave your arms and legs" speech. She did eventually shave everything down, and I'm not gonna lie, I was relieved. I realize now that was pretty shallow of me, but my thirteen-year-old self was just happy it was gone!

We talked for a lot of hours about the things that were different in Holland compared to South Dakota. One of them was drinking. There wasn't a drinking age in Holland, and she had been drinking for several years by the time she got to us in little rural South Dakota. She got a big kick out of trying to show me the hand motions you needed to do to order a beer in a pub over there. I must have looked as funny as she did trying to master the Midwest habits, lingo, and actions.

She introduced me to rum, and there was no looking back. I'm not sure how she got a bottle of it since she was only seventeen when she lived here, but she knew I hated beer. I guess she knew me well enough to have a gut feeling for what I would like. I felt somewhat left out with friends, not even being able to fake my way through one beer. It just triggers the gag reflex in the back of my throat every time. She said I have just the thing for you. A few nights later, she showed up with rum mixed with Coke, and I was sure she had just delivered me the best-kept secret in the world. It became my thing, and everyone knew that if I showed up at a "kegger" holding a bottle of Coke, there was likely some type of rum in there. It was almost my signature thanks to my foreign sister.

After that introduction and my proclaiming that rum was now my drink of choice, one of my dad's hired hands provided a small bottle of Bacardi under the driver's seat of my car each weekend. Not sure if he thought I had promised something in return for that rum, but he never demanded payment in any form. He was just the Rum Fairy!

Along the way, someone decided it was always super cool to put some kind of Schnapps into hot chocolate during the winter and into iced tea during the summer. One late summer night, I found myself on all fours in a parking lot saying hello again to all of the Peach Schnapps I had drunk earlier with some sweet tea! Saying hello going down and hello coming back up are two totally different life experiences. I'm not peaceful, nor am I a graceful puker. I think I remember it shooting out of every opening in my body. It felt like that stuff was even coming out of my ears it left my body so forcefully! For thirty years, I never had anything peach—not even hand soap. But this last summer, my boss handed me a glass of peach tea, and I had taken a sip before I was alerted that there was anything in there. Surprisingly, I held it together, and I didn't even hate it!

I didn't make it out of high school without my fair share of Lucille Ball Moments. Most of them are a blur of embarrassment because the self-rejection was so new and at the highest pendulum swing in the cycle at that point. Luckily for me there was no social media. I would've had a really hard time getting over myself if some of those things would have been shared on social media at that point. Dad always insisted on a curfew of midnight. Freshman year or senior year, it didn't matter, midnight was all the later he wanted to give. I was ridiculously awful at making curfew. When my dad said midnight, he did not mean 12:01 a.m. he meant no later than 12:00:00 a.m.

Mom, please stop reading my book at this point. You may continue on to the next chapter.

I was always trying to stay at whatever party there was until the last second possible and then push the limits of my guardian angel, physics, and any other rule of law. I absolutely know God has a plan for me because I survived probably thousands of moments death was chasing me home. Six of those miles home were paved highway, but the rest were gravel roads. Depending on whether the county had just worked those roads determined how dangerous they were for speeds in excess of 80-90 mph. The winter of my sophomore year was especially treacherous, and snow packed. If you don't live in the upper Midwest, you may not be aware of the fact that when blizzards set in, we don't stay home for twenty-four hours prior to the snow. We do our thing. That being said, there were many nights I would be coming home, racing to make curfew after the snow had drifted over the road, making snow drifts. Well, up to a certain point, you just kind of ram them with your vehicle and keep going.

The first incident I remember that winter was me sneaking up on midnight. I left town at twelve minutes until midnight. I had thirteen miles to go in drifted snow. Hush with the math and the logic running through your brain, I thought I could make it. And I almost did. I made it 12.75 miles and turned the last corner, which was technically on our property, so I could've argued I was there at midnight, right? Anyway, our property had two driveways with the house being on the second. I got past the first driveway, and there between the two, I hit a snowdrift that wasn't going to let me win. I hit it, and my car went to a screeching, immediate stop. Looking at the clock, it was 11:59 p.m., and I did not want to spend the next several weeks at home. I slammed that sucker in park, opened my door, and began running for all I had to reach the front door. At 12:01 a.m., I busted through that front door with all of the quiet nature of a bull in a china closet heaving and wheezing. I was met with the familiar sight of my dad in his rocking chair, eyes red from waiting up on me, and an extended silence.

"Young lady, why are you breathing like you just ran home from town?"

"Well, you see Dad, I would have been here before midnight I swear! But my car got stuck so I had to run." I said, still doing that forty-year-old smoker wheezing impression.

The serious gaze continued. "Heather Marie, where is your car?"

Me: "Oh, between the driveways out here."

He sighed. "You just left your car out stuck in the middle of the road?"

Not quite understanding why he was asking such a question, I said "Uh yeah! I had to make curfew!"

His head drooped, and he heaved a big sigh, but I was pretty sure I saw a little smirk at my predicament being hidden when he dropped his head with that sigh. He called my brother to help him go pull my car out, and when we got there, both of them looked at me like I was some extraterrestrial alien because I had just left it running. I still don't understand what the problem was. I knew we were going to go get it immediately! Anyway, we pulled it out, and everyone was in bed before 1:00 a.m. again. He either let me slide, or all of the chaos made him forget because I didn't get grounded on that one.

Right now, I need to give a shout-out to my oldest brother for that winter. I wasn't his child, just his little sister, and yet ten times that winter, I found myself in the ditch for different reasons. I have a really good explanation for each and every one. They got to where they didn't want to hear what they were, but I had reasons! That winter was really bad, and I had a Monte Carlo that was pretty loose steering. I never could get the touch of driving that dang thing in the snow, and it gave me great pleasure once to watch my dad get stuck in that car as well. With a "Not one word Heather," he got out to push, and I slid over to the driver's seat.

The other significant snowy ditch event that year, I was at a movie party after a basketball game that required me take the back roads home. Dad was forever telling me not to take the back roads, but I really didn't want to leave early enough to go all the way around, so testing fate once again, I headed home about fifteen minutes before curfew. The snowplows had not gotten to the back roads during this storm and wow did I find myself in a pickle. The ice pack under the snow and the drifts was a bad combination for this ditzy gal, and I ended up not only off the road but pretty dadgum far out into the ditch, almost into the next field. South Dakota blizzards have claimed their fair share of lives, so Dad always made sure I was prepared with survival needs. In the trunk was a down-filled sleeping bag, some beef jerky, and some peanut butter.

There were no cell phones back then. I just had to hope Dad hadn't fallen asleep and would notice that I didn't make curfew and would come looking for me. Having complete faith in my dad and brother to take care of me and never let me die, I wrapped myself up inside that down sleeping bag, turned the car off, snacked on a couple beef jerky sticks, and went to sleep. By the way, all of these are no-no's for blizzard survival skills—except turning off the car. My exhaust was covered in snow, so I knew I had to turn it off to stay alive or something.

When they found me, they were none too happy. I wasn't supposed to be on the back roads. With my car off, there were no taillights or headlights to help them find me, and it made the search pretty stressful for them. As stated before, having complete faith in them, I had no stress—until Dad and my brother and I were standing in the snowbank that had a hold of my car and my dad shouted, "Heather Marie, have you been drinking?"

Straight-up fear shot out my vocal cords. "No sir!" I mean after all, it took them several hours to find me and I had only had one drink at the party . . . It was long out of my system, and I felt that was the loophole I was looking for.

"Well young lady, I do not understand how someone can just drive off the road and make it across a steep ditch almost into the field!"

I replied, "I may have been going a little too fast on that corner."

That didn't help my cause. My brother still gives me grief about that winter to this day, and all I can do is giggle and say "I'm sorry! Thank you though!"

Considering my teenage Peach Parking Lot Puke Party (yuck!) and my driving record, it was very hard for the sixteen-year-old version of myself to justify arguing for a later curfew with my dad when he said, "95 percent of the time, anything you're out doing after midnight is going to be illegal or immoral. Now convince me why you should be out after midnight?" Yes sir . . . that would be correct, but can I still have an extra hour for my curfew? I had nothing. There wasn't a good argument for that kind of logic.

Well, shoot . . . Why was he so good? Why was he so creative showing his smarty-pants knowledge anyway? This man! He was total frustration, total inspiration, and I couldn't do without him. Little did I know that most men are exactly this way and only the best ones will be a "forever" part of your life.

He had a creative way to deliver most of his parenting moves. I discussed whether I should share this story with my husband because it was a bit embarrassing for both of us. He reluctantly said I could share anything. I'll probably have to remind him of this later, but he did say "Fine. Yeah, share it."

I already told you that I met my husband as a thirteen-year-old freshman in high school. Eventually, we started dating in the second half of my freshman year. Remember that early high school is a time when hickeys start making an appearance. All of the less experienced girls had that love/hate relationship with them. We kind of thought they were trashy, but at the same time, we kind of wanted one! So eventually there came a night when I had drunk a little too much of the bottle of rum from the Rum Fairy. While with my boyfriend (now my husband), I was just inebriated enough that it didn't even cross my mind to say no when things progressed a little farther than ever before, and I came home that night with a hickey on my neck. I thought I had just done an A-1 job of hiding it. Neither Mom nor Dad mentioned anything. I had achieved a new level of awesomeness with all the other girls at school, and the making out it took to get there wasn't so bad at all! I was going to get out of this whole thing without even being in trouble! I thought I had made it. I had not, in fact, made it . . .

Tuesday night came along, and there was a home boys basketball game. Corey and I walked over and said hi to Mom and Dad when they came in. We bantered a little small talk, and when we went to go sit in the student section, my dad stopped Corey and handed him a lollipop. He looked at my dad, and then at me, and then back to my dad again.

"Just in case you ever get the urge to suck on something again: use that, not my daughter." My dad kept a level face while delivering the most creative, maybe the most impactful parenting move I'd ever seen him pull in all my years. Not threatening or comical, just a dead-level straight face. Corey and I both blushed ninety-five shades of red. He put the sucker in his coat pocket, choked on the words "yes sir," and we awkwardly spun on our heels to head for the student section. Corey and I never spoke about it again. It was too embarrassing. To this day, it's another moment from my life where I can still feel my jaws react as they did in the moment. I'm pretty sure my mouth couldn't have been wider open when he delivered that little one-liner.

When I became a parent, I was always looking for ways to be able to deliver an impactful lesson with creative new ways to discipline. I gained half of my parenting tactics from my parents and the other half from Clair and Heathcliff Huxtable from *The Cosby Show*. I know that Bill Cosby has disappointed us in the recent past, but back when my ideas of parenting were being formed, we didn't know all of that, and the creative ways he talked the Huxtable kids through things or disciplined his kids was very impactful on me.

Back to drinking: it's always such a struggle. Should I drink? Should I not? All kinds of people and church denominations have their own "rules" regarding this activity. I've heard so many women my age refer to this bucket list item as an honest-to-God epiphany. Ready?

"When I found out I could have a glass of wine and love Jesus, my whole life changed!"

Um, your whole life, really?

I mean, yes, it's true. I could drink in moderation and love Jesus. Whether I should or not is another decision just between him and me. I'm going to leave that one up to God and each individual.

The only time I can unequivocally say I should never ever consider drinking is when I'm in the company of someone with an addictive personality disorder. If I'm with them, I should always have the compassion and gentle spirit to not do something that would make them tempted. Otherwise, if God hasn't laid down any "Thou shalt nots" in my life regarding this, then I guess I'm good to go. But getting to this point took a long time of shaking off organized church legalism and seeking God about whether it was a heavy "No" for everyone or if it was another case-by-case relationship issue with him.

When you're underage and in your parent's home: it's a steadfast no. As an adult though, when I think of the amazing peace and freedom, I get from talking to (only) God about stuff I am allowed to do and stuff I am not allowed to do . . . Well, it's my prayer that every person actually reaches toward heaven for all of their answers and not a flesh and blood human that God has a different life story for.

CHAPTER 11

EXPERIMENTING WITH SELF-CARE

I had the privilege of turning fifty during the year of the COVID-19 pandemic. The bat meat disease. Wait, wait, maybe it's the chemical warfare disease, the "China Virus" (Come on, you heard the word "China" in Donald Trump's voice, didn't you?), the birth mother to social distancing: What names did you give it? Apparently, it isn't "woke" to make fun of the situation, but if being woke or politically correct means we can't laugh during the most stressful time of life, I don't want to be a part of that life!

In Oklahoma, we didn't close down as much as some parts of the nation. I did teach the rest of the year from home via virtual learning. If you think keeping the attention of four-year-old preschool kiddos is tough in a classroom, you should try it in front of a computer. Good grief!

There's only so much sitting around the house I can do, only so many Netflix series I can watch, only so many board games and Facebook Live moments I can do. At some point in a pandemic where everyone is being asked to stay home,

I had to find other things to do, things that preferably can't be finished in a day. I began to take advantage of all the extra time to do things I liked to do! I organized and nailed down a skincare routine, I tried lash extensions and hair extensions for the first time. Girl, yes! I just bought cheap hair extensions from Amazon.

Let me chase this squirrel for just a minute! First of all, let's address the lash extensions. Beautiful lashes are my thing! At fifty, I am now contemplating an eyelid reduction because my eyelids appear to be the first thing to have headed south, and they've done so in waves: first one layer and then a second. They just fold right over on top of each other like a waterfall, and they're beginning to mess with my lashes! I see women walking around everywhere with everything from beautifully positioned and natural-looking enhancements to full-on caterpillars on their eyelids! It's all accepted and considered normal now! (*Insert clapping and whistles here!*) Approaching this scenario gave me a little anxiety though because my own lashes were great. They're just blonde, so you can't see them much without mascara. This is what gave birth to the idea of lash extensions! They're already black so you wake up stunning, right? Right?

The problem is these Lucille Ball Moments that plague me. All I can imagine is that when they decide to let go, it will be like my cheek said, "Red Rover, Red Rover, let all the lashes come over," and all at once, there will be a departing like the Children of Israel running through the Red Sea and every false lash will all be sitting on my cheek at the same time, waving awkwardly at whomever I'm talking to. That, or one entire eye will shed every false lash at once into my iced tea while having lunch with a friend, and the other eye will be proudly standing erect, not about to let go for another week! I have Lucille Ball(ed) my way into so many similar situations, I really, really have to plan for all contingencies when approaching something new.

Fears extinguished, I made my first appointment for lash extensions when the lockdown was lifted, and we could do such things again. The before-and-after pictures with my eyes closed looked amazing, but when looking into a mirror, they didn't really look full enough. I spent the next two weeks seeing them fall out everywhere. Two fell in the shower, and you'd better believe I dropped to my knees and rescued them from the jaws of the drain so I could glue them suckers back on with glue from good ol' Walmart!

I did a fairly good job keeping up with them, (even though gluing them back on yourself is not supposed to be part of the plan) until I didn't, and y'all let me tell you something: I looked in the mirror and felt like Yzma from *The Emperor's New Groove* was looking back at me! Yzma is a pencil-thin woman with very sharp features: sharp cheekbones, very sharp shoulders, and a pointy nose. She wears a V-neck purple dress with a slit in the thigh that only accentuates her thin, harsh features. The one thing she kind of, well sort of, has going for her are her lashes. They are exceptionally long. It was maybe her only feminine feature. The problem was that she only has like four or five really, terribly long lashes, and most of them stick out in different directions. When I looked in that mirror what I saw was that only the longest ones had stayed on and there were like six of them. Somehow, they all decided to point in different directions. Before I panicked, I half giggled and had this terrible urge to yell "Kronk! Pull the lever!" But I knew my husband would not play the part nor see the humor in it, so I stood there staring at my predicament.

I sort of became fixated on it. I'm the same way about fingernail polish. If it's chipped, it all has to go. No matter where I am or if I have nail polish remover or not. I'll sit there and scratch all of it off with a car key or whatever else is within reach. So, as I stared at myself, things began to take on an urgency to get it fixed. Now!

I called Tiffany and made an appointment for a fill. She ended up having to cancel twice, and by then I was in a full-on panic mode. These buggers were hanging on for dear life, and I just couldn't have this anymore. My solution to the problem? My husband. You'll find he is the solution to many of my problems—as he should be. I called him into our bedroom, and he found me lying sideways on the bed with my head hanging slightly off the edge of the bed. "Please take these tiny nail scissors and just cut the four false lashes on each eye down to the same length as the natural lashes so that I can be put out of this misery."

With a shrug of his shoulders, he said okay and grabbed his headlamp. Listen to me closely: if I ever tell you my husband has helped me with a "procedure," please always imagine him with a headlamp on. It's just his thing. I questioned him as to how long this seemingly short procedure was taking and he replied, "You want me to do a good job, don't you?" He seemed very disgusted. Knowing that he was probably frustrated at me not being able to wait for another appointment, I hushed. After all, not many husbands would agree to all the things he agrees to in order to tolerate all my crazy whims. When I know I'm being a tad "extra," I try to be as pleasant as I can. But he was taking a really, really long time to cut five or six exceptionally long lashes on each eye, and it was bugging me.

When he got done, I went to look in the mirror. Y'all, I wanted to cry. How in the world did six lashes create the situation I saw in the mirror? I had no lashes left. It was like as they were all shedding off; my natural lashes broke off at the eyelid or about halfway up! I could barely feel any lashes on my eyes! My beautiful (but blonde) eyelashes were gone, and now so were the six Yzma lashes! I really, really should have immediately caught on, but I didn't. So, I marched myself down to Walmart (wearing a mask) with no eyelashes and bought the cheap glue-on one-strip eyelashes until I could figure out if my natural lashes would ever grow back.

This process is not anywhere near as easy as one might expect. That glue got everywhere! By the time I finally got them to stick on (albeit unevenly), my waterfall eyelids were glued together, no longer gliding up and down as they used to, and I was probably the spitting image of a drug addict with my eyes bugging out everywhere because I'd glued them up near my eyebrows.

I grabbed the coconut oil and removed everything. "Honey! I'm going to need your help with eyelashes again!" He was really good at this procedure. Even and symmetrical between both eyes with minimal glue application! Atta boy, honey!

After all of the panic and chaos, I sat down and thought through all of the events of the day regarding my eyelashes. Can anyone else figure out what dawned on me at that moment? What actually caused my natural lashes to come up missing? My husband had cut all of my natural lashes when he was only supposed to cut the four Yzma lashes!

When this epiphany hit me, I marched myself into the living room where he was watching an old rerun of NASCAR (Lord give me strength) and yelled, "You cut my natural lashes?" He jumped a little on the couch, obviously fearing for his life, and began to plead his case.

"They were uneven! I was just trying to even them up, and I kept having to go shorter and shorter and shorter! I'm sorry!" Y'all, if I hadn't figured that out on my own, he would have never confessed! I thought the weight of artificial lashes had caused them to break off. Not true: he had kept cutting them layer by layer until he got to my eyelid. The fact that Mr. Westover is still walking the earth and married to me after that one is a straight-up miracle.

The hair extensions were much less traumatic. I purchased a set for thirty-five dollars from Amazon because I figured if we are all okay with women having caterpillar eyelashes that are obviously false, it shouldn't matter if you can tell that the hair extensions are synthetic! I like them. During application, there comes a moment when you sit a little taller and feel like you probably need a fresh coat of lipstick: red lipstick. My hair is so fine that it breaks off easily, and I've never been able to grow my hair out very much because of this. Having the added length did kind of make me feel like a hottie patottie. But I've also decided they are only for occasions where I want to have a long ponytail. They make my head itch too much to have them on every day. I did not need to ask my husband for help. It all seemed like a win-win on these things. I could wear them when I wanted and leave them hanging in the bathroom when I wasn't feeling it. I'd just gained all kinds of ridiculous confidence in these do-it-at-home self-care procedures and stepped out way too far on the next one.

For the grand finale, (You're going to die, and I can't believe I'm confessing all of this to you) I wasn't done with trying new self-care procedures. For the previous thirty years,

I was always raising a herd of children and chasing their dreams (Well, at least we were chasing some of their dreams, the rest of them were chasing their wants). When the last one from my first set of kiddos was born, they were six, four, two, and a newborn. I had my hands full. So of course, when the oldest one was eleven, we adopted a fourteen-year-old boy! Makes sense, right? We had five kids, all running or chasing softball, volleyball, wrestling, or some other dream they may have had. I didn't even have the money to have my hair professionally done on a regular basis until sometime in my late thirties. If I would have had the money, I for sure wouldn't have had the time.

For my fiftieth birthday in July, we decided that we were all going to go to the ocean together. All of the travel restrictions were beginning to be lifted, and we decided to just pray and go. Being well aware of COVID-19, we did what we could to take precautions by booking condos where we could cook for ourselves and limiting our activities to all outdoor events where we wouldn't be in a cramped space with other potential COVID-19 carriers. But nevertheless, we were going! Four of my daughters were able to make it with us, and all my grandchildren came as well. Preparing for this trip, there were multiple swimsuits and cover-ups purchased along with sandals, sun hats, sunglasses; the list went on and on.

When I received the swimsuits, I decided, you know what? I'm turning fifty! There shouldn't be any personal thing I want to be done that I should have to decide against. So Brazilian bikini wax, here I come! I had had my eyebrows done once or twice over the years but never a bikini wax.

I set out to introduce the idea to my husband who promptly vetoed this. He said he wanted no man or woman beside a doctor seeing or messing with me "down there" and he certainly wasn't going to pay someone else to be "down there" either.

That's cute and all but, I don't take no for an answer easily. I try to take his preferences into consideration when it's something he feels strongly about, but I wasn't giving up.

After thinking of my dilemma for a while, I got on Amazon and ordered him an at-home wax kit. When it arrived, I called him into the bedroom, smiled my biggest smile, and proceeded to say, "I know how you feel about me getting a bikini wax with someone else, so I got you a gift. Get ready big boy, you're about to become an esthetician and do my bikini waxes yourself!" I handed him the box and told him he might need to Google how to do Brazilian bikini wax so that everything would be handled properly. I wanted him to have some prior knowledge about the subject so we could avoid another eyelash scenario.

The next night, I crawl up on the bed completely . . . Hm, how should I explain this? I crawl up on the bed completely "exposed." The wax had been melted and strategically placed on the nightstand.

Remember when I told you to visualize my husband wearing a headlamp for every procedure he has done for me? Eyelashes, splinter removal, foiling my hair (yes, he's tried his hand at this for me as well), and now, bikini wax. He approached me hesitantly with this headlamp on, which instantly brought on a migraine because he likes himself a strong headlamp. I covered my face with a towel and told him to just get started.

He had melted the wax to a temperature just below that of the surface of the sun, and I did not think to check it. When he dropped a giant glob of that wax onto my tender skin that had never experienced anything like this, I immediately gasped out loud and came halfway off the bed.

"What are you doing?" I shouted.

"Well, I wanted it to be good and melted, so I turned it up on high!" he shouted back. "What's wrong? Are you okay?"

I couldn't yell at him; I was busy trying to remember my Lamaze breathing to get through this pain. I made sure the towel was back over my face, and when I recovered, I growled from beneath that towel, "Turn it down. It just has to be runny. It does not have to be brought to a boil."

The first wax strip removal not only removed hair as it was supposed to, but it also removed about seven layers of skin because the temperature of the wax that had been turned on so high that it just burned right down into my netherlands layer by layer.

If you would have been sitting in the living room that night, you would have heard lots of heavy breathing, a few moans, a couple screams (muffled by the towel), both of us shouting the other's name occasionally, and finally, me saying "Just get it done already Corey" and him replying, "Okay, I'll hurry!"

What would have traveled through your mind would not have been even close to the shenanigans going on behind that closed door, but when we were done, I had the bikini wax I wanted. He did a great job, and the blisters even healed up before we made it to Florida!

There are a lot of women who would have given up after the eyelash fiasco with their husband, but the eternal optimist in me is always positive: "This time, it'll be fine!" I'm sure this is a properly decent genetic trait in me that somewhere along the way got warped a little because the fact that I never give up even long after I should have just keeps getting me into so much trouble!

The next time I have a bright idea, I don't think I'm going to ask him first. I think I'm just going to go do it: Pay whomever and just come home with something new accomplished on my body. Unless he asks questions, I'm not revealing anything!

CHAPTER 12

MAKING THINGS HAPPEN AFTER 50

I want to be on offense when it comes to living out the rest of my life. I want to do things regularly to drive some of the events that happen for me, to call out a play and hopefully, move ten yards further down the field to where I want to be. Sometimes though, you bust through the line and there are even bigger gains waiting for you on the other side. A lot of people that I've talked to are happy to just wake up each morning and see what comes. That's not me. It's probably a really good thing because people like them likely have less stress in their life than I do. Some of the things I plan are just a whole roller coaster all on their own!

I definitely put things in motion. I never really called them a bucket list until I started getting older. For example, singing has always been a part of my life. While raising my children, I simply didn't have time to participate, but I had always tried to attend and loved every second of the concerts put on by the Singing ChurchWomen of Oklahoma. There is just something about singing with such a large choir with hundreds of voices harmonizing and using their talents for the God they believe in.

The year my fourth daughter left for college I tried out for and became a member of this fantastic group. I tried out after one of their concerts held in a local church. Pretty much the auditions consisted of singing up and down the scales to see what kind of vocal range you had and whether you had control over your voice. Once that was over, they had you sing a favorite hymn while someone harmonized with you and then you harmonized with them in return.

Normally, one would have received a letter confirming whether your audition had been successful or not. I tried out in the fall. My acceptance letter didn't come out until the following summer, about mid-June. I knew I was a decent singer, so I couldn't figure out what I might have done. A friend of mine who was a member of the group kept telling me that unless I had received a rejection letter, I should hang in there. June took a very long time to come, but when I saw the letter in the mailbox, I was almost too afraid to open it. The wait had created such anxiety it had me very nervous. To open the letter and find "Welcome to the Singing ChurchWomen of Oklahoma" was a huge relief and a big moment of celebration.

Later that fall I was able to travel with this group to New York City where we stayed right on Times Square. We had traveled there together because we had been invited to perform in Carnegie Hall on the Perelman Stage with none other than Christian recording artist Sandi Patty. Also performing with her was the group Veritas. They had about three hundred of us squished onto that stage backing them up. I never entered the hall through the front doors one time throughout the whole experience. Some of the ladies went through the front doors just to look, but I knew this was a special opportunity that may never come again. I wanted only a specific set of events to be my memories from Carnegie Hall. I am maybe one of very few people in the world who only knows what Carnegie Hall looks like from the stage. When we left for the venue, we always entered from a side street in the back and went into a dressing room off of the stage. We left all of our personal items in the dressing room and were ushered up through a side door to the stage.

When we walked up on stage for the first time, there was a hush. None of us was willing to break the history, the beauty, and the majesty of that moment. After giving us just a second to acclimate, we heard the click of the conductor's baton as he called our attention. He smiled at us, knowing he was about to give us the moment of a lifetime. "Let's just do this thing. We will practice in a minute." He told us what song to sing, and we began the once-in-a-lifetime experience together. The acoustics in that hall were something like I've never experienced before and maybe will never experience again. Carnegie Hall almost echoes your singing. When we would cut off a refrain, it sounded like the ivory-colored Renaissance-style walls and red velvet seats just sang the notes back to us for a second or two. It really moved my soul.

Isaac Stern once claimed, "Everywhere in the world, music enhances a hall, with one exception; Carnegie Hall enhances the music."

They announced an opportunity for anyone who had their music memorized to be able to move up to the first standing row. I'm not ashamed to tell you that although I had all of the words memorized, the notes were a little iffy. But to have the opportunity to be in the first standing row meant I would have full view and get to have the full experience. They watched several of us to be sure that we in fact had all of the words memorized and eventually put me in the front with several others. I love making eye contact with people in the audience as I sing, and being in that row just increased my chances dramatically. I like to see what parts of the music move them. I like to see their body involuntarily sway when their soul melts into one with the orchestra and singers.

Between myself and the lady from the Bronx who also had been invited to join the choir, we were able to hit all of the alto 1 notes and be each other's strength when the other wasn't so sure. I'll probably never see her again, but I really did love the whole experience with her.

When I realized that I was one of the few people in the world who only knew what the view looked like from the stage, I purposed in my heart to never go sit in the audience. The experience from the stage is more than enough. So many greats have performed before me, and so many will perform after me. How did I ever get the chance to be standing here? The boisterous Lucille Ball disaster who always flew by the seat of her pants standing on the Perelman Stage of Carnegie Hall singing about God to a packed house: unbelievable. Right before the concert began, we prayed together as a group. Everything went exactly as we had prayed for and practiced. The concert was a wonderful success.

We also went on a dinner cruise out to the Statue of Liberty together and danced to the Electric Slide on the ship's dance floor as the skyline of New York City passed us by. I don't remember if Sandi Patty participated, but the gentlemen of Veritas tore up the dance floor with us. Having the NYC skyline float gently past, lit ablaze by the setting sun was yet another once-in-a-lifetime experience I'm so grateful to have gotten on this trip. All of the experiences seemed to fit perfectly together even though they couldn't have been more different.

We had a twenty-four-hour hop-on/hop-off pass on specific tour buses. Even though it was the week before Thanksgiving and a little nippy out, I took a seat on the top of the bus so I could see everything perfectly. There was a moment I felt like I was actually in a Batman movie with the particular building that loomed just ahead of us. It was so breathtaking. There were cathedrals that were so architecturally distinct, I could have stood and just studied them for hours. But my absolute favorite sighting in NYC was miniature stained glass water towers randomly placed on rooftops all over the city just for the beauty of it. They moved me, and I set about trying to find a replica in every gift shop in walking distance, yet not one store carried them. Maybe I'm just moved by things that aren't the societal norm. Who knows, but I would like to go again and see those water towers.

Sunday morning, we attended worship services at the Brooklyn Tabernacle so we could see their choir in person. While there, Lucille Ball made an appearance when I passed out from low blood pressure. They carted me off to the side of the sanctuary and sat me down on the floor up against the wall while they found someone in the medical profession to attend to me. By the time they returned, I was told I had slumped over on the wall, taking on the look of a person who had celebrated too hard rather than a patient, but I was doing the best I could. The doctor concluded that an event the night before with the lights in Times Square had started an ocular migraine that was playing havoc with all of my body, including my blood pressure.

On Saturday evening, we had been exploring the square. When we left our hotel, the M&M building was our first stop across the street. When I looked up at the signage above their building, their sign was so extremely bright that as I stepped off the curb, I closed my eyes real tight and grabbed the friend next to me. When I looked up again to the blinding sign, a glitch caused it to go completely black, and while I was still looking at the black screen it came on twice as bright as before.

I closed my eyes again, and when I opened them, I was temporarily blind. My eyes just wouldn't work at all for about three minutes. There was a tiny bit of panic, but eventually, I blinked, and my eyesight popped right back as it should be. The rest of the evening I felt a little off and definitely had a headache, but I functioned fine until I got in the middle of the Brooklyn Tabernacle the next morning—a little embarrassing but survivable.

Since then, I've recorded a couple of CDs with this group. By the time this book is printed, I will have traveled to Nashville, Tennessee to record another. This is what I mean by driving my life. That one decision to finally join SCW of Oklahoma has brought so many opportunities and wonderful memories into my life: things I would have never experienced if I hadn't put myself out there and joined. There are always secondary blessings that get attached to individual adventures.

At this point, I try to stay alert with eyes for blessings. When I hear of an adventure that sounds interesting, I go for it. I realize that none of this would be possible without a husband like mine. It took us twenty-five years of marriage to realize that there just wasn't going to be a good compromise where adventure was concerned. Corey doesn't like change or being away from home. I don't like things to stay the same and have a need to wander. We spent those twenty-five years believing that we couldn't travel, vacation, or adventure without each other if we were going to be a respectable married couple. But with every adventure I expressed interest in, he would stare at me for a while before shaking his head in disbelief and just walking away. Finally, one night over a plate of fajitas, we hashed it out.

He decided that for him to attain the level of happiness that he always thought he wanted, he should stay home. He also decided that making me do it with him was draining the life and sparkle from my eyes.

I have referred to my Gypsy blood more than once in this book, and I feel like I should let you in on why I say that. My dad's ancestors were from Germany and the United Kingdom. My mom's are from Germany and Bohemia. In both of the locations in Germany and Bohemia that I've looked up, there were significant groups of Gypsy nomads. Call me crazy, but I'm convinced they are definitely part of my bloodlines. My husband believes it anyway, and maybe it makes it just a little easier to tolerate this crazy need for adventure that flows in his wife.

We started out slowly at first, but to be honest, since turning fifty, I've probably been able to travel more than any one person should be allowed to. I love him for sensing that the Gypsy blood cries out when being stationary for too long and it must be appeased. I know that not all marriages or partners would sense it or care, and I'm so grateful he does. Each year, he commits to two vacations: one with our daughter who is still a child in the home for the traditional "family vacation," and one just with the two of us around the time of our anniversary.

Our anniversary trips have taken on somewhat a life of their own. We alternate years and one of us gets to decide where we go and what we do. Our destinations absolutely follow our personalities. Typically, when it's my turn to plan the anniversary, it involves some kind of palm tree and the sound of the ocean waves. When he picks, we typically load up the four-wheeler and stay in the backwoods of Oklahoma somewhere fishing, hiking, and using survival skills of some sort. People assume I hate the years he gets to pick, but I really sincerely don't. I love seeing him happy, and I love being a part of those kinds of things with him. Besides, I'm a farm girl; we know how and enjoy doing these things as well.

The first year he got to pick, we ended up along the Arkansas River in some ol' boy's hunting cabin that seemed to be held together on the outside by the yellow spray foam that poofs out everywhere. It made me raise an eyebrow, telegraphing my uncertainty in Corey's direction, but once we got inside, it had all been remodeled and was pretty luxurious for a hunting cabin. I had bought myself (Ahem) a beautiful long stem yellow rose at the grocery store on the way. I drained my drink, used the bottle as a vase, and stocked the fridge with our groceries. It seemed acceptable, and I was appeased.

A little later, I walked out the side door to a snakeskin shed close to four feet long. I honestly think there was more fear in Corey's eyes the second I pointed it out than there was in mine. He knew this had the potential to go sideways very quickly. We did a meticulous search around the cabin, turning over rocks and running my walking stick through all the tall grass. He kept saying, "Heather once they shed, they go to a new location. They don't stick around, I promise."

I absolutely knew his promise was a bold-faced lie. It was self-preservation for the weekend he so desperately wanted. So, I sucked it up and pretended to believe him. I can do that now because I am at least a little better about snakes, remember? But I absolutely know that creepy, gave-me-the-willies-just to think-about-it-thing lived under the crawl space of that cabin. I silently begged God to reenact our pact since I had already held a snake and battled my fear and all. "Please God, just don't let him come out, and if he absolutely must, don't let me see him. Amen."

CHAPTER 13

THE SECOND HALF OF MY LIFE

During the year of COVID-19, I had plenty of time to reevaluate my priorities, to examine whether the second half of my life was going the way I wanted—or at least as close as possible to how I wanted it to play out anyway. I want to be able to be intentional about the things I spend my time on. As I was nearing fifty, one of the thoughts that kept rolling around in my head was: This is it. I don't get any of this back, and there are no do-overs. Whatever I do today is what will forever go down in history as all I did today. If I spend it lying on the couch, that seems like a real waste of time considering I now have less time on earth than I have already lived.

Definitely, on my bucket list is travel. That's pretty broad and something I would be doing regardless of my age since my husband works for a major airline and our travel benefits are amazing. Our options are kind of limitless there.

I have a short list of adventures that I would like to be able to experience. Exploring any of our National Parks would be fun; America really has some of the best sights to see, and we probably couldn't get through them all in a lifetime. I would like to explore the Mayan ruins in Mexico and the ruins in Machu Picchu. Exploring castles in Scotland, along with touring my ancestors' lands in Germany are also destinations of interest. Maybe the one single event I'd love to experience is to sleep in a glass igloo to watch the northern lights in Iceland. Once I wake up in the morning though, I'd like to be bound for some tropical hiding spot because I don't like the cold. Even though I don't believe in past lives, if there were, I'm positive I would have been a pirate. Don't ask me why. I don't even know. It's just something I think I'd have gotten caught up in if I lived back then, and tropical places make me feel at home.

One of the other things I'd like to improve on is entertaining. By entertaining I mean to intentionally have people over to just hang out and create memories with them. My husband is a self-proclaimed hermit. He doesn't want people to come over very often. We bought a little place with five acres out on the dead-end of a dirt road for a reason! No one can find us, not even Google. Every time I try to invite someone out or get Google to fix our location, he questions my sanity. Who in their right mind would want everyone and Google to know where you live? But there was a time where we had a really big house that was perfect for entertaining, and we did it all the time. He was a little more tolerant of it back then I guess.

Between letting the kids have a revolving door for their friends, friends of ours who came over quite often to play spades, and countless kids from the youth group we let camp out on the floor, I also had family gatherings regularly. I miss that. I love the activity, the noise, the laughter, and the memories.

A few years after my dad passed away, we invited all my siblings over for Thanksgiving, and I wanted it to be a big deal because my mom and my little sister were coming down from South Dakota and I knew that it needed to be a great event for her. All her kids would be under one roof, and I couldn't wait for that to happen for her.

Remember that being in the kitchen and cooking for her family was my mom's entire life. She was looking forward to doing this again. After making homemade brown gravy, we kicked her out of the kitchen. Somehow, I got it in my head that it would be a wonderful gift to her, to kick her out of the kitchen so she could sit in the living room with her boys and grandkids watching football. I mean, that's what I would have wanted! I am not her; she is not me.

We had roughly thirty-five people there that day. We also had a large fireplace. Several in the family looked at that large fireplace and assumed it needed a large amount of wood. My husband said he spent the day following people around pulling logs out of the fire after they put them in and before it could really catch fire. Someone else in the family decided Mom should watch *The Patriot* with Mel Gibson instead of football, and this was also a regrettable decision in her eyes.

Mom's feathers were ruffled, and she wasn't really enjoying her time in the living room. I could hear her sigh with annoyance, and I was pretty sure I had seen tears at one point that she was trying to keep from falling. My feathers were ruffled because she wasn't appreciating the gift I had just given her of not having to slave over the stove for a holiday meal. The tension was thicker than that dang gravy of hers. I had pulled my sisters, sisters-in-law, nieces, and daughters into the kitchen and we had divided and were conquering all the necessary dishes for a good old fashion holiday meal like the Waltons would've had around their table. Until...

We were nearing the finish line. I had removed the pan of green beans from the stove. My sister pulled the glass pan of homemade rolls from the oven and placed it on the (still hot) empty burner spot on the stove and we were finishing the last few tiny details when my kitchen exploded. It was a full-on explosion. Every woman in the kitchen froze. Some of us felt the debris hit our hair, face, and arms. We looked back and forth at each other trying to assess what might have happened. I have never seen a group of women have bigger eyes and mouths more wide-open than that moment right there. Suddenly, my little sister screamed, "Heather! The rolls!"

When the explosion happened, my mom says everyone in the house jumped and froze. They really thought there was a real explosion with a gas line or something because it was so loud. A few people headed for the front door. About that time, my husband barreled into the kitchen from one direction and my little sister's husband entered from another direction. She met hers at that door and I leveled "the look" on mine.

"Get out! And do not let Mother in here!"

Corey: "Is everyone okay?"

Me: "Out!"

Now all the women went back to staring at each other with big eyes. The glass pan of rolls had exploded, throwing glass all over the kitchen. The corn was ruined, the rolls were ruined, and for the love of God, the brown gravy had glass floating on the top of it. In my panic, the thought really ran through my mind that if I just got my mouth down there, maybe I could suck the glass right off the top of that gravy and Mom would never know the difference.

Realizing that everything had to be thrown away and knowing that it was already going to be a late lunch and by now everyone was probably pretty hungry, I also knew that there was no way we had time for our yeast rolls to be remade. My niece worked at a local restaurant that served yeast rolls and although they were closed for that day, she had a key to the building and went to grab a tray from there so we could have dinner rolls. The rest of us set to work making new corn and other things we had lost on that stove, but there wasn't any replacing that dadgum brown gravy.

As I'm writing this book, I'm sitting in my mom's living room, and she just reminded me twice how dry that turkey was because there was no gravy. Remember I've turned fifty years old already and my mom is reminding me how dry that turkey was twenty plus years ago. It was a big event on the family Richter scale. I don't think we actually got to eat lunch until about 4:00 p.m. that day . . . which was another thing that ruffled feathers, but there was nothing I could do about that. To this day, there isn't a person there who doesn't immediately laugh so hard they cry when that holiday is brought up. We even had to sweep glass up from the far reaches of the laundry room. Lesson learned: do not pull a glass pan out of an oven and set it on a still-hot burner—ever. So much chaos. And that dang brown gravy . . .

I hope to have a big house again, one that will hold big families and big love. I want Christmases and Thanksgivings and 4th of July's, holidays, and random Saturdays that everyone is running all over my house together, where the disasters are hilarious and we all end up around the table eating turkey without gravy just like the Waltons—or as close to it as we could anyway—and where we pray before the meal, even if we had just been screaming at each other to get out of the kitchen and not to let Mother anywhere near that door!

I want to surround myself with family and friends consistently, but maybe my "such a time as this" moment is for more as well. I really want to reach others. I want to reach out to the middle-school-age kid who maybe has been the object of a social media "burner account" where really unflattering pictures are taken and posted of them. It's not so far from the "I Hate Heather Nuttall Club" experience. Pictures taken unaware are most of the time the last picture you want on social media. With every comment, every like, and every emoji, your heart sinks deeper. You put on a brave face and say it doesn't bother you, but inside, you're noticing, internalizing, and grieving.

I want to share my story and encourage those who need it to get professional counseling. Counseling can help you develop tools to combat rejection, self-loathing, poor body image, anxiety, depression, self-inflicted isolation, and so much more. I'm praying that you can utilize these tools for combat decades earlier than I did, that you find your self-worth in the unconditional love of a parent, that you believe in your immeasurable worth in God's eyes, and that you begin to see your worth in your own. It doesn't matter what mistakes you've made or are making. Your last failure is not who you are. It's not even where you are anymore, right?

Sharing what using those tools looks like in my life so that the spouse of an addict can look at us and find hope is something my heart longs for. Implementing these tools in your life and your marriage will look completely different than they do in ours, but they are what will help you find your feet. When you're in the middle of this particular hell, you feel like you're hanging on, and you are, but there are things happening to you that you probably don't think you have time to address. You feel like your life is on fire around you, and you just have to keep going. For everyone else's sake, you must keep going. The truth is, you're on fire too. You're just so focused on the next hour, the next minute, and the next second for those you love that you can't see it.

Sharing hope for tomorrow not just with faith in God, but in the daily potholes of life is something I long for. I don't want to be your example. Please don't follow my Lucille Ball self. I just want to be your diving board, the one who helps springboard you into your era of overcoming whatever is behind you clawing at you to keep you back.

There is hope. There is help. You just need to admit it, mostly to yourself, and reach out for that help. Help may actually come in the form of a friend group, a pastor, spiritual leader, or a licensed counselor. Whichever direction you go, of course, be sure you can trust their experience, their heart, and their methods. There are just as many people who have been hurt by spiritual leaders and licensed therapists as there are people who have been let down by friends. The point is, if it doesn't feel right, keep going. Find a new therapist; they aren't one size fits all. Find a new spiritual mentor; they aren't all spiritual victors. Ask God, just like my grandmother said. Ask God, and keep asking God until you have an answer, direction for action, and peace. In a world focused on the moment of becoming the victim, reach to become the victor.

ACKNOWLEDGMENTS

To Eric Koester, the one with the vision to create this program Creators Institute Inc., thank you for following your vision and pouring it into so many authors. The encouragement and wisdom you shared are invaluable.

To everyone at Creators Institute, Developmental Editor Katie Siegler, and the May 2022 writing cohort, I have gained so many friends, and I am looking forward to reading so many new books starting in June! Thank you for bouncing off ideas, keeping me on track, and reassuring me every time the imposter syndrome hit me hard.

To the professionals at New Degree Press, I truly am in awe of the well-oiled, amazing, and professional machine that New Degree Press is. You've supported us and kept us moving, you've helped us reach our campaign goals to cover publishing costs and fees, and you've created the most fun and artistically perfect covers for each of us. It is amazing. Thank you.

Last but not least, to my Marketing and Revisions Editor Kathy Wood, I honestly feel like I've found my soul sister. You're professional, real, compassionate, and able to give me a kick in the pants all at the same time. Not many people are able to be all that with me, yet you "handle" me like a pro. Your friendship will always be valuable to me. Much love and respect Kathy!

~Heather Nuttall Westover

To this list of my supporters, my brothers and sisters in arms, my cheering section, and the ones who lift me up when I fall: May I be able to do the same for you during your finest moments in life someday. Much love and respect to all of you.

Eric Koester, Megen Cohea, Monica Thacker, Cindi Hemm, Darcie Kringen, Carly Manning, Sarena Beastrom, Juanita Nuttall, Randy Warne, Shelly Chute, Curtis Peery, Jo DeGeer, Darcy Henry, Dana Young, Denise Loveless, Sandra Griese, Andrea Pointer, Angel Galvan, Dana Hess, Sabrina Miller, Sara Mumy, Erin Davis, Char Squires Keller, Shelly Slavin, Kent Carver, Canbrilynn Robinson, Brenda Lamb, Andrea Hunt, Jessica Garrett, Cathy Garrett, Karen Hester, Susan Rainez, Kayla Steifel, Dianne Shaw, Tiffany Bailey, Jamie Lakey, Michelle McCullough, Kimberly Bolewski, Annika, Russell-Manke, Shane Hilmer, Leslie Hillsberry, Christina Nuttall, Rhonda Gipson, Amanda Frailey, Lesli Colestock, Ken & Andrea May, Lea Nance, Vicki Hilton, Keith Sparks, Kim Rogers, Wendy Haddock, Cathy Oxford, Jada Olmstead, Lori Woodall, Holly Crivolio, Nikki Dunn, Cassandra Beaudet-Kirby, Andrea Hudson, Teri Hartman, Amy Holland, Monica Ross, Lindsey Eisenhauer, Ashley Leavitt, Dom Anglin, Christina Tate, Monette Clark, Skylar Miller, Maghan Spring, Margie Cravens, Glynda Hunt, Pam Agee, Belinda Stevenson, Martha Hoffman, Brittany Binger, Patricia Harper, Lisa Miller, and Cheri Wittler.

APPENDIX

CHAPTER 1

WB Kids. "Looney Tuesdays | Iconic Duo: Wile E. Coyote & Roadrunner | Looney Tunes | WB Kids." March 31, 2020. Video, 21:57. https://youtu.be/Aewj-OwcMlo.

CHAPTER 2

Famous Biographies. "Trisha Yearwood Biography." May 20, 2019. Video, 5:48.
https://youtu.be/fHZKdRLoMok.

Fathom Event. "I Love Lucy: A Colorized Celebration—Job Switching." July 19, 2019. Video, 2:15.
https://youtu.be/K3axU2bodDk.

Going the Distance: The Rocky Series Podcast. "Rocky Balboa—Rocky Remembers Adrian." December 18, 2019. Video, 4:11.
https://youtu.be/aP4F7WM3YoY.

MLB. "Red Sox DH David Ortiz Elected to Hall of Fame." January 15, 2022. Video, 13:16.
https://youtu.be/qxZA9tH1wBg.

The Chef's Kitchen. "Legal Seafood in Boston." January 24, 2011. Video, 4:55.
https://youtu.be/XTwaFU_woXg.

WatchMojo.com. "Garth Brooks: Biography of the Country Singer." February 7, 2012. Video, 6:45.
https://youtu.be/F5p0_JaKGHU.

CHAPTER 5

Classic TV in 4K. "4K HEE HAW." January 28, 1970. Video, 36:46.
https://youtu.be/3bUCg46mVjE.

ElTerribleProduction. "Top 10 Muhammad Ali Best Knockouts HD #ElTerribleProductions." November 9, 2014. Video, 5:52.
https://youtu.be/C_fEIVwjrew.

Farm Aid. "Tanya Tucker—Delta Dawn (Live at Farm Aid)." October 16, 2019. Video, 4:55.
https://youtu.be/XwjGvD2ezik.

Ret-O-Vision. "A Charlie Brown Christmas Special." December 4, 2017. Video, 45:52.
https://youtu.be/m7dqZ6Jy-GE.

YouTube Movies & Shows. "The Wizard of Oz (1939)." July 18, 2020. Video, 2:55.
https://youtu.be/EsbZflqNVag.

YouTube Movies & Shows. "True Grit (1969)." June 2, 2012. Video, 3:40. https://youtu.be/XYkkZDpnKss.

<subtitle>Chapter 6

Sockiethesock. "Thumper, What Did Your Father Tell You?" April 17, 2011. Video, 1:35. https://youtu.be/Pi8f9g8-Wpc.

TheNBAHistory. "Wilt Chamberlain's 100 point Game". March 2, 2011. Video, 4:28. https://youtu.be/LxMeEzhvNRs.

CHAPTER 7

Paramount Pictures. "Pet Sematary (2019)—Official Trailer—Paramount Pictures." October 10, 2018. Video, 2:02. https://youtu.be/VllcgXSIJkE.

CHAPTER 8

Martha Stewart. "Martha Stewart's Chocolate Pots de Creme (Pudding) | Martha Bakes Recipes." February 9, 2022. Video, 4:33. https://youtu.be/AHPt61z9Xys.

Movieclips. "A Nightmare on Elm Street (1984)—Tina's Nightmare Scene (1/10) | Movie Clips." October 9th, 2018. Video, 2:54. https://youtu.be/HcrTqof683A.

Sara Gillette. "June Cleaver on Women's Changing Rolls in the 1960's." March 16, 2014. Video, 1:12. https://youtu.be/IgIPcOdnyxA.

CHAPTER 9

Movieclips. "Raiders of the Lost Ark (4/10) Movie CLIP—The Well of Souls (1981) HD." May 5, 2016. Video, 2:29. https://youtu.be/c6XHLe94SJA.

Chapter 10

BillCosby. "The Cosby Show Theo Earring." May 9, 2017. Video, 3:21. https://youtu.be/5nbDVUT-nO.

CHAPTER 11

Nation. "Donald Trump Calls Covid-19 the 'China Virus'—FILE." March 19, 2021. Video, 3:50. https://youtu.be/opjsx94m8qA.

YouTube Movies & Shows. "The Emperor's New Groove." April 24, 2012. Video, 2:23. https://youtu.be/PaKn5-06a6s.

CHAPTER 12

Baptist General Convention of Oklahoma. "Singing ChurchWomen | BGCO Worship and Music." 2022. https://www.bgcoworship.org/groups/scw/.

Carnegie Hall. "Live with Carnegie Hall: Isaac Stern Centenary." July 21, 2020. Video, 1:00:01. https://youtu.be/xZgGli6gDHE.

Gaither Music TV. "Sandy Patty—Duets Medley (LIVE) ft. Veritas." June 15, 2017. Video, 7:35. https://youtu.be/hd169ZK_v_0.

CHAPTER 13

Nostramos. "The Walton's Final Goodnight." August 12, 2013. Video, 2:28.

https://youtu.be/u7q6mswocHs.

YouTube Movies & Shows. "The Patriot (2000)." June 29, 2013. Video, 2:39.

https://youtu.be/WdWuLtcBme4.